BREAD BAKING
revised edition

Lou Seibert Pappas

Bristol Publishing Enterprises
San Leandro, California

A Nitty Gritty® Cookbook

©1992 Bristol Publishing Enterprises, Inc.
P.O. Box 1737, San Leandro, California
94577.

Printed in the United States of America.

ISBN 1-55867-042-4

Cover design: Frank Paredes
Cover photography: John Benson
Food stylist: Stephanie Greenleigh
Illustrator: Mike Nelson

CONTENTS

INTRODUCTION 1
FACTS AND TIPS ABOUT MAKING BREAD 4
PLAIN AND WHOLESOME LOAVES 12
BRIOCHE AND EGG BREADS 39
SPECIALTY ROLLS 62
INTERNATIONAL HOLIDAY BREADS 98
SOURDOUGH BREADS 136
DESSERT BREADS 149
INDEX 169

INTRODUCTION

My love for bread baking stems from my heritage. My maternal Swedish great-grandparents owned a thriving *bakeriet* in Gothenberg, Sweden, at the turn of the century. The sparkling windows were a showplace filled with golden brown tea rings, swirled cinnamon twists and family-style white and orange-rye loaves. There was delectable Spritsar, apple cakes and marzipan tarts, as well.

As a new bride in the Pacific Northwest, Grammy Helgesson carried on the baking tradition, producing big panfuls of sugar-glazed cinnamon rolls and 6 to 8 plump white loaves at a time for her large family. The children would race home from school and cut "heels" to frost with freshly churned butter and homemade wild berry jelly.

My German *Grossmutter* Seibert cloaked her granite dishpan of rising dough with a fur throw. Her breads were more robust in character, emphasizing the local Eastern Oregon stone-cut grains in dark and crusty rye, whole wheat and pumpernickel varieties along with her holiday specialty, an almond and honey-glazed Bienenstich.

My mother combines both legacies with her own knack for blending grains, deftly turning out countless varieties of whole grain breads, beautiful caramelized sticky rolls and orange-frosted brioche cakes in rich succession.

Now I carry on the tradition, interweaving the decorative breads from the Greek family into which I married with my own. Yaya's glorious anise-scented Christopsomo and lemon-imbued Easter Tsoureki are now integral to our holiday celebrations. The many international breads sampled on my travels have since been perfected and savored at home.

Our family "baking tree" emphasizes how bread making is a composite of lore, love and skill — plus a touch of magic, perhaps — passed down through generations in homes throughout the world.

The sensual delight of producing a loaf of bread and sharing it with family or friends is a joyful and rewarding experience for all. When my children were young, often I would divide a piece of dough with them. Shaping the Danish Kringler was their specialty. Their young hands reveled in the soft, springy feel of dough. They loved watching it balloon in size. And most of all, they cherished its warm goodness. The tantalizing aroma and delectable taste of freshly baked bread offer pleasures hard to surpass. Turning out an honest loaf is not difficult once you master a few basic techniques.

Bread baking dates back to the Stone Age. It began in earnest when many turned from a nomadic hunting life to a more settled existence which allowed for the cultivation of grain. The first bread was an unleavened wafer-thin cake, baked on hot stones. The Egyptians turned bread baking into a skilled craft.

Their bread was leavened with yeast-rich foam scooped from the top of fermenting wines. Breads in variety were found in the tombs of the pharaohs. Some were flavored with camphor, others with sesame and poppy seeds. Much later the European baker was prized as an important tradesman. Today many view this skill as a satisfying means of self expression and the art of bread baking is experiencing new popularity.

This collection of breads, garnered through family traditions and worldly travels, was first introduced in 1975. More than 200,000 readers later, popular demand has encouraged me to produce this revised version of the original book, with old favorite recipes updated, and with some new additions I hope you will enjoy.

Lou Seibert Pappas
Palo Alto, California

FACTS AND TIPS
ABOUT MAKING BREAD

INGREDIENTS

Flour. Wheat flour, the major ingredient in bread, contains a protein substance called gluten. When wheat flour is combined with liquid, then stirred and kneaded, the gluten stretches to form the elastic network that holds the gas bubbles formed by the yeast. Bread flour is the highest in protein and is desirable for bread making, but it must be thoroughly kneaded. White all-purpose flour is wheat flour. It is available both bleached and unbleached. The latter is preferable because it is a sturdier flour and is desirable because it has not been whitened with a chemical agent. Whole wheat flour has less gluten than white flour and whole wheat breads are generally heavier and smaller. Rice and soy flour have no gluten, so are unsatisfactory by themselves for making yeast breads. Because the amount and quality of gluten are never exactly the same, the amount of flour needed will vary. Temperatures and humidity can also affect the absorption properties of flour and the time needed for beating and kneading will vary for the same reason. With a little experience, a breadmaker will learn to recognize when the mixture "feels" right.

Special grains and flours such as rye, cracked wheat, buckwheat, soybean, rice, corn meal and wheat germ all add variety, character and extra nutrition to breads. Most need to be combined with all-purpose flour because they lack enough gluten to effect a proper bread structure.

Leavening. Yeast, the leavening agent most commonly used in bread making, is a living plant which grows in warm, moist doughs. It gives off bubbles of gas, causing the dough to rise. Yeast comes in two forms, active dry and compressed, which produce equally good results when used in the conventional mixing method of dissolving the yeast in warm water (85° to 95° for compressed; 105° to 115° for active dry). Only the dry form can be used in the easy-mix method where it is mixed with part of the flour, then the liquid is added and the mixture beaten with an electric mixer. This method requires the water to be warmer, between 120° and 130°.

The temperature for dissolving compressed yeast should never be more than 85° to 95°. A word of caution — if the liquid used in dissolving the yeast or adding to yeast mixtures is too hot, it will kill the yeast and the bread will not rise. A candy thermometer is the most accurate way of testing the water temperature. One package, about 1 tablespoon, of active dry yeast is interchangeable with one 0.6 ounce cake of compressed yeast. Active dry yeast is less perishable than the compressed cakes which must be refrigerated. To determine if a cake of yeast is usable, crumble it between your fingers. If it crumbles easily, it's still good.

Liquids. The kind of liquid used in bread making influences the final product. Milk gives a soft crust and creamy white crumb. Breads made with water have a crisper, thicker crust such as found in French bread. Unpasteurized milk needs to be scalded to destroy a particular enzyme which causes "gummy" bread. Pasteurized, evaporated or reconstituted dry milk need only be warmed enough to activate the yeast.

Sugar. Stimulates the yeast to produce gas, helps the crust to brown and adds flavor. The sugar is usually in granulated form, but brown sugar, molasses or honey may be used.

Fat. Butter, margarine, olive oil or vegetable oil makes breads tender, gives them a soft silky crumb and aids in browning. They also add flavor.

Salt. Not only enhances flavor, but is necessary to control the growth of the yeast, making the dough rise more slowly for a better texture.

Eggs. Add a golden color and rich flavor and make the crumb fine and the crust tender.

Nuts and Fruits. Add flavor and variety, but slow the rising time.

TIPS AND TECHNIQUES

Preliminary mixing. Strong beating to develop the gluten should be done with an electric appliance or by hand using a wooden spoon. Either way, add half of the specified amount of flour, or as much as your machine can easily handle. (When using a heavy duty mixer, such as a Kitchen Aid, it is wise to attach the splash cover to prevent the flour from flying out as it is added to the bowl.) Beat the mixture hard for a few minutes. Add the rest of the flour when you knead the dough.

Hand kneading. Preferably do this on a board, but if necessary you may use a counter top or table. Sprinkle the surface with flour and rub some on your hands. Shape the dough into a ball and place on the floured surface. Using the heels of your hands, push the dough away with a rolling motion. Fold it toward you. Then turn the dough one quarter turn around. Continue the sequence of pushing, folding and turning, making a rhythmic motion. Repeat until the dough is smooth, satiny, elastic and no longer sticky, adding more flour when necessary. Allow at least 10 minutes for kneading hand-mixed doughs. Machine mixing reduces kneading time considerably. To test if dough is kneaded enough, make an indentation with your finger. The dough will spring back when it is kneaded enough. Ample kneading creates bread with a springy texture and maximum volume. Extra kneading does not harm the dough, but enhances it.

Machine kneading. It is possible to totally eliminate hand kneading by using a heavy duty mixer such as a Kitchen Aid, Kenwood or Robot Coupe, a food processor or an electric pasta maker, to do the kneading for you. For the electric mixer, use the dough hook and knead for about five minutes. Add just enough flour to cause the dough to cling to the dough hook. For the pasta maker or a small food processor, first mix the ingredients together in a bowl and then place half at a time in the machine and knead until it is smooth and elastic, about 1 minute for the food processor and 5 minutes for the pasta maker. For a large capacity food processor, all the dough of a small batch can be mixed and kneaded in one step.

Regardless of which machine you use, no hand kneading is required. Just place the kneaded dough in a greased bowl.

Greasing the bowl. Rub the bowl with a thin film of butter, margarine or oil and turn the dough in it so it is greased on all sides. This prevents a crust from forming during rising.

Rising. Select a draft-free location for the dough to rise. An even temperature of about 70° to 75° is best for all but refrigerator-type doughs. If your kitchen is not warm enough, you can create a warm place in any of these ways:

- Set the bowl of dough in a cold oven with a large pan of hot water beneath it.

- Set the bowl of dough in an oven with the oven light on.
- Heat an electric oven to warm; then turn the heat off. Check to make sure the oven is not too hot, and then place the bowl of dough in the oven with the door slightly open.

Testing. To tell when the dough has doubled, press two fingertips lightly ½ inch into the dough. If the indentation remains, the dough is ready for shaping.

Punching down. Push your fist into the center of the dough. Pull the edges of the dough to the center, turn dough over and remove to a lightly floured surface. Knead a minute or two to remove air bubbles.

Shaping. For a loaf of bread, start by dividing the dough as specified in the recipe. Shape into a smooth ball. Stretch the top surface of the dough, pulling it underneath to make a taut, smooth surface. Tuck ends underneath.

Testing for lightness before baking. Touch lightly with a finger. It should fee "poppy" — light and springy.

Glazes. Just before baking, the risen dough is often brushed with a glaze to give it a special finish when it is baked. The various glazes include water, lightly beaten egg white, egg yolk beaten with 1 tablespoon milk or water, cornstarch mixed with water, and cream. Each results in a slightly different finish.

Baking. Preheat the oven. Allow ample room for the heat to circulate around the pans. If tops of loaves begin to over-brown, lay a piece of aluminum foil loosely over the top of each one. To test for doneness, tap or rap the top of the loaf with your knuckles. If it sounds hollow, it is done.

Cooling. As soon as the bread or rolls are baked, remove from pans to a wire cooling rack. When cool, package in plastic bags, tie securely, and store at room temperature or refrigerate or freeze.

Freezing. Breads freeze beautifully when packaged air-tight in plastic freezing bags or wrapped in foil and sealed with tape. Label and date the packages. To reheat, let thaw completely at room temperature, wrap in foil, and heat in a 350° oven 20 to 30 minutes, or until thoroughly heated. It is wise to leave breads unfrosted if you plan to freeze them. Frost just before using.

COPING WITH PROBLEMS

Bread that doesn't rise. When bread dough refuses to rise after a considerable time span, what should you do? You've probably killed the yeast, perhaps by combining it with liquid that was too hot. The best solution is to dissolve 1 package of active dry yeast and 1 teaspoon sugar in ½ cup warm water (110°). Mix in ½ cup all-purpose flour. Let stand in a warm place for 10 minutes, or until spongy. Beat this mixture into the unrisen dough. Then knead in enough additional flour to correct consistency. Proceed as usual by placing the dough in a warm spot to rise.

Bread that rises too much. What should you do when the shaped loaves of dough have risen too much in the pans before they are baked? You can turn the dough out on a floured board, knead lightly and reshape into loaves. Place in greased pans and let rise again just until doubled, and then bake.

Punching down. How often can you punch dough down before shaping it? It is quite all right to let the dough rise twice and punch it down twice before shaping it. Remember, dough rises more quickly each successive time it rises and is punched down. It is important to punch the dough down as soon as it has doubled in size so the texture will be fine-grained, rather than coarse.

No time to finish. What should you do if you have mixed the dough and then are not free to complete the rising and baking sequence? Let the dough rise once, punch it down and refrigerate it, covered with plastic wrap. Later, either the same day or the following one, remove the pan from the refrigerator and let the dough rise in a warm place until doubled in size. Shape, let rise and bake.

PLAIN AND WHOLESOME LOAVES

QUICK HONEY WHITE BREAD . 13

BASIC WHITE BREAD . . . 14

WHOLE WHEAT BREAD . . . 15

CHEDDAR CHEESE BREAD. . 15

CINNAMON SWIRL BREAD . . 15

RAISIN BREAD. 15

FRENCH-STYLE WHITE BREAD 16

DATE PECAN BREAD. . . . 17

WHOLE WHEAT COFFEE CAN
BREAD 18

HEALTH BREAD 19

CHEESE WHEAT BREAD . . 19

MIXED NUT BREAD 20

ROASTED GARLIC LOAVES. . 22

PEASANT POTATO ROUNDS . 24

ANADAMA BREAD. 26

SAN BENITO HOUSE MOLASSES
BREAD 27

GRAMMY'S ORANGE BREAD . 28

NUT BREAD 30

RUSSIAN BLACK BREAD . . 32

VARIETY BREAD 34

FOUGASSE 36

FOCACCIA 36

QUICK HONEY WHITE BREAD

Makes 3 loaves

This recipe goes together fast in rapid-mix style.

7 to 8 cups unbleached all-purpose
  flour or bread flour
1 cup nonfat dry milk powder
3 pkg. active dry yeast

1 tbs. salt
3 cups warm water (125°)
⅓ cup soft butter or margarine
⅓ cup honey

Place 2 cups flour, milk powder, yeast and salt in a large mixing bowl. Pour in water and beat 1 minute using an electric mixer. Add butter and honey. Beat 1 minute longer. Gradually add enough remaining flour to make a soft dough. Beat well, using a heavy duty electric mixer or wooden spoon. Remove to a lightly floured board. Knead 5 to 10 minutes, or until smooth and satiny. Place in a greased bowl and lightly butter top of dough. Cover with a clean kitchen towel and let rise in a warm place until doubled in size, about 1½ hours.

Punch dough down. Turn out on a lightly floured board and knead gently a minute or two to remove air bubbles. Divide into 3 pieces. Shape into loaves and place in 3 greased 9-x-15-inch loaf pans. Cover with a clean kitchen towel. Let rise in a warm place until doubled in size, about 35 to 40 minutes. Bake in a preheated 375° oven 40 to 45 minutes, or until golden brown and loaves sound hollow when thumped.

BASIC WHITE BREAD

Makes 2 loaves or braids

This wholesome bread is extremely versatile. Five delicious variations, which follow, can be made from this basic recipe.

2 pkg. active dry yeast
1 cup warm water
1 cup milk
3 tbs. sugar
2½ tsp. salt

3 tbs. butter
5 cups unbleached all-purpose flour
  or bread flour
egg glaze: 1 egg white beaten with
  1 tbs. water

Sprinkle yeast into warm water and let stand until dissolved. Heat milk and pour into a large mixing bowl containing sugar, salt and butter. Cool to lukewarm. Stir in dissolved yeast. Add 3 cups flour and beat 5 minutes. Gradually add enough remaining flour to make a soft dough. Turn out on a lightly floured board and knead until smooth and no longer sticky, about 10 minutes. Place in a greased bowl and butter top of dough lightly. Cover with a clean kitchen towel and let rise in a warm place until doubled in size, about 1½ hours.

Punch dough down. Turn out on a lightly floured board and knead gently a minute or two to remove air bubbles. Divide in half and shape into loaves. Place in 2 greased 9-x-5-inch loaf pans. (Or, divide each half into thirds. Roll each piece into a rope, and braid. Place on greased baking sheets and continue as directed for loaf pans.) Cover with a kitchen towel. Let rise in a warm place until doubled in size, about 45 minutes. Brush tops with egg glaze. Bake in a preheated 375° oven 40 to 45 minutes, or until brown and loaves sound hollow when thumped.

WHOLE WHEAT BREAD

Substitute 2½ cups whole wheat flour and ¼ cup wheat germ for 2¾ cups of the all-purpose flour specified above.

CINNAMON SWIRL BREAD

Let basic dough rise once. Punch down and knead a minute or two on a lightly floured board. Divide in half. Roll into 15- x 7-inch rectangles. Spread each one with 1 tablespoon soft butter. Combine 6 tablespoons sugar with 2 teaspoons cinnamon. Spread half of mixture on each rectangle. Roll tightly as you would a jelly roll, beginning with narrow side. Place in pans to rise in a warm place until almost double, about 35 to 40 minutes. Bake at 375° 40 to 45 minutes or until done.

RAISIN BREAD

Follow basic recipe. After mixture has been beaten 5 minutes, stir in 1 cup raisins and enough remaining flour to make soft dough. Proceed as directed.

CHEDDAR CHEESE BREAD

Let basic dough rise once. Punch down. Knead in 1½ cups grated, sharp cheddar cheese. Divide in half and shape into rounds. Place in 2 greased 9-inch round cake pans to rise in a warm place until almost double, 35 to 40 minutes. Bake at 375° 40 to 45 minutes.

FRENCH STYLE WHITE BREAD

Let basic dough rise once. Punch down and knead lightly. Divide dough in half. Shape into 2 long loaves. Place on greased baking sheets and let rise in a warm place until doubled in size. Make diagonal slashes with a razor blade about 2½ inches apart. Brush with water. Bake at 375° 40 to 45 minutes or until done.

DATE PECAN BREAD

Makes 2 loaves

This spicy fruit bread is exceptional sliced and spread with natural cream cheese and orange marmalade.

2 pkg. active dry yeast
3 tbs. sugar
2½ tsp. salt
2 tsp. grated orange peel
½ cup nonfat dried milk powder
1 cup whole wheat flour

5 cups unbleached all-purpose flour
  or bread flour
2¾ cups warm water (125°)
3 tbs. soft butter
1 cup pitted, chopped dates
½ cup coarsely chopped pecans

Place yeast, sugar, salt, orange peel, dried milk, whole wheat flour, and 1 cup flour in a large mixing bowl. Stir in very warm water (125°). Beat until smooth. Mix in butter and enough remaining flour to make a soft dough. Stir in dates and nuts. Turn out on a lightly floured board and knead until smooth. Place in a greased bowl. Cover and let rise in a warm place until doubled in size.

Turn out on a floured board and knead lightly. Divide dough in half and shape into 2 loaves. Place in 2 greased 9-x-5-inch loaf pans. Cover and let rise until doubled. Bake in a preheated 375° oven 35 to 40 minutes or until loaves sound hollow when thumped. Remove from pans and cool on wire racks.

WHOLE WHEAT COFFEE CAN BREAD

Makes 2 loaves

Coffee cans make neat round containers for baking bread. The baked loaves come out of the cans with ease — simply turn them upside-down.

3 cups unbleached all-purpose flour
  or bread flour
3 cups whole wheat flour
1½ tsp. salt

2 pkg. active dry yeast
2½ cups warm water (125°)
¼ cup brown sugar
¼ cup butter

In a large mixing bowl, stir together 1 cup unbleached flour, 1 cup whole wheat flour, salt, yeast and brown sugar. Stir in water. Beat until smooth. Mix in butter and remaining whole wheat flour. Beat 5 minutes longer. Gradually add enough of the remaining all-purpose flour to make a stiff dough. Turn out on a floured board. Knead 5 to 10 minutes, or until smooth and no longer sticky. Place in a greased bowl and butter top of dough lightly. Cover with clean kitchen towel and let rise in a warm place until doubled in size, about 1½ hours.

Punch down and turn out on a lightly floured board. Knead a minute or two to remove air bubbles. Divide in half and shape into 2 round loaves. Place in

2 greased 2-pound coffee cans or 2 greased 9-x-5-inch loaf pans. Cover with a kitchen towel. Let rise until doubled, about 35 to 40 minutes. Bake in a preheated 375° oven for 40 to 45 minutes, or until loaves sound hollow when thumped.

CHEESE WHEAT BREAD

Follow the recipe for *Whole Wheat Coffee Can Bread*, except mix 1 tablespoon dried oregano and 2 cups shredded cheddar, Jarlsberg or Swiss cheese into the dough after it has risen once. Continue as directed.

HEALTH BREAD

Follow the recipe for *Whole Wheat Coffee Can Bread*, except substitute ½ cup wheat germ for ½ cup all-purpose flour.

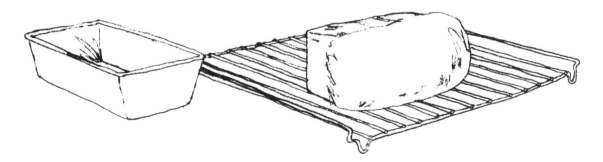

MIXED NUT BREAD

Makes 1 loaf

This bread slices beautifully, revealing the assorted nuts which stud each slice. It makes a stellar bread to offer with a cheese tray for dessert.

1 pkg. active dry yeast
1/4 cup warm water
3/4 cup milk
3 tbs. butter
3 tbs. sugar
1 tsp. salt
1 egg
2 3/4 cups unbleached all-purpose flour
   or bread flour
3/4 cup roasted, salted mixed nuts
   (do not chop)
1 egg white, lightly beaten

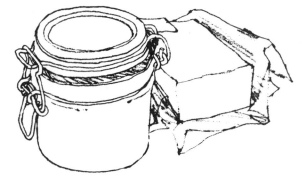

Sprinkle yeast into warm water. Stir until dissolved. Heat milk and pour over butter and sugar in a large mixing bowl. Let cool to lukewarm. Stir in salt, egg and dissolved yeast. Gradually add enough flour to make a soft dough, beating well after each addition. Mix in nuts. Turn out onto a lightly floured board. Knead until smooth, place in a greased bowl, and butter top of dough lightly. Cover with a clean kitchen towel and let rise in a warm place until doubled in size, about 1½ hours.

Punch dough down and turn out on a floured board. Knead a minute or two to remove air bubbles. Shape into a flat cake. Place in a greased 9-inch round cake pan, cover and let rise in a warm place until doubled, about 35 to 40 minutes. Brush with beaten egg white. Bake in a preheated 350° oven 35 to 40 minutes, or until loaf sounds hollow when thumped.

ROASTED GARLIC LOAVES

Makes 2 loaves

Roasted garlic imbues its sweet, caramelized flavor to this savory loaf. It is ideal for sandwiches or as an accompaniment to cheeses and meats. It's excellent toasted as well, served spread with chevre and topped with soft sun-dried tomatoes and a basil sprig for an appetizer.

1 head or about 8 cloves garlic
⅓ cup olive oil
2 pkg. active dry yeast
2½ cups warm water
3 cups unbleached all-purpose flour
   (approximately) or bread flour

2 cups whole wheat flour
2½ tsp. salt
¼ cup honey

Rub the unpeeled garlic with 2 tsp. olive oil, place in a small baking dish and bake in a 325° oven for 40 minutes or until soft. Let cool. Sprinkle yeast into ½ cup warm water (approximately 105°) and let stand until proofed, about 10 minutes. In a large mixing bowl, place 2½ cups flour and salt. Add remaining water, honey and olive oil, and mix well using a heavy duty electric mixer or beat with a wooden spoon. Mix in yeast, stir in whole wheat flour and add enough remaining flour to make a soft dough. Knead with dough hook for 10 minutes or turn out on a lightly floured board and knead by hand. Place in a bowl, cover and let rise until doubled in size, about 1½ hours.

Sqeeze the soft garlic from its skin. Punch down dough and turn out on a lightly floured board. Mix in half the garlic. Divide dough in half and shape into 2 long loaves, kneading out air bubbles. Place on a lightly greased baking sheet, spacing several inches apart. With a finger, poke about 6 to 8 holes in the top surface of each loaf. Fill with garlic, dividing evenly. Cover and let rise until doubled. Brush with olive oil. Bake in a preheated 375° oven for 35 to 40 minutes or until golden brown and loaves sound hollow when thumped. Let cool 10 minutes, remove from pan to a wire rack and cool completely.

PEASANT POTATO ROUNDS

Makes 1 loaf

Mashed potatoes keep bread moist and make it age well.

1 pkg. active dry yeast
1¼ cups warm water
1½ cups rye flour
¾ tsp. salt
¼ cup molasses

1 cup mashed potatoes
1 tbs. caraway seeds
1¾ cups unbleached all-purpose
  flour or bread flour
Cornstarch Glaze

Sprinkle yeast into ¼ cup warm water. Let stand until dissolved. Add remaining 1 cup water, 1 cup rye flour, salt, molasses, potatoes and caraway seed. Beat well. Gradually add 1 cup all-purpose flour and remaining rye flour. Beat until smooth. Beat in enough all-purpose flour to make a soft dough. Turn out on a lightly floured board. Knead in remaining flour. Place in a greased bowl, butter top of dough lightly and cover with a clean kitchen towel. Let rise in a warm place until doubled in size, about 1½ hours.

Punch dough down. Turn out on a floured board, and knead a minute or two. Shape into one large round. Place in a greased 9-inch round pan or casserole. Cover and let rise in a warm place until doubled in size, about 35 to 40 minutes. Bake in a preheated 375° oven 40 to 45 minutes. Brush with *Cornstarch Glaze* the last 10 minutes of baking. The loaf should sound hollow when thumped.

Cornstarch Glaze

Bring ¼ cup water to a boil. Blend in 1 tsp. cornstarch which has been mixed with 1 tbs. cold water. Boil, stirring constantly, until thickened.

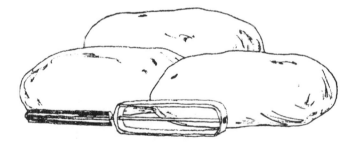

ANADAMA BREAD

Makes 2 loaves

This old-time New England corn meal bread is pleasantly sweet. It is especially good toasted and spread with marmalade or apple butter.

5 cups unbleached all-purpose flour
 or bread flour
1 cup corn meal
2 pkg. active dry yeast

2 tsp. salt
2 cups warm water (125°)
5 tbs. soft butter
½ cup molasses

Stir 2 cups flour, corn meal, yeast and salt together in a mixing bowl. Add water, butter and molasses. Beat hard for 3 minutes. Mix in enough remaining flour to make a stiff dough. Turn out on a floured board. Knead until no longer sticky. Place in a greased bowl, butter top of dough lightly and cover with a clean kitchen towel. Let rise in a warm place until doubled in size, about 1½ hours.

Punch dough down. Turn out on a floured board and knead a minute or two. Divide dough in half. Shape into 2 balls. Place in greased 9-x-5-inch loaf pans. Cover and let rise until doubled, about 35 to 40 minutes. Bake in a preheated 375° oven 45 to 50 minutes, or until loaves sound hollow when tapped.

SAN BENITO HOUSE MOLASSES BREAD
Makes 1 loaf

The charming San Benito Restaurant and Inn in Half Moon Bay, California, is famous for its crusty deep brown bread. the 8-x-12-inch-long loaves are baked daily, a dozen at a time. Here is an adaptation of the recipe.

1 cup warm water
1 pkg. active dry yeast
2 tsp. brown sugar
1½ tsp. salt
⅓ cup dark molasses

⅓ cup canola oil
2 cups unbleached all-purpose flour
  or bread flour
1½ cups whole wheat flour

In a large mixing bowl, place water, yeast and brown sugar. Stir gently and let mixture stand for 20 minutes in a warm place until bubbles have formed on top. Mix in salt, molasses and oil. Gradually mix in 1½ cups unbleached flour and the whole wheat flour. Turn out on a floured board and knead in remaining flour until dough is smooth and elastic.

Place in a bowl, cover with plastic wrap and let rise in a warm place until doubled in size. Turn out on a floured board and shape into a long loaf. Cover and let rise until doubled. Bake in a preheated 300° oven for 1 hour and 15 minutes.

GRAMMY'S ORANGE BREAD

Makes 3 loaves

Shreds of orange rind punctuate this wholesome four-grain bread.

2½ cups water
1 cup oatmeal
2 pkg. active dry yeast
2½ tsp. salt
zest from 1 orange
⅓ cup butter
¼ cup molasses
1 cup warm milk
1½ cups barley flour
1 cup rye flour
3 to 4 cups all-purpose flour

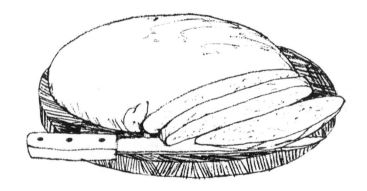

Place 2 cups water and oatmeal in a saucepan. Bring to a boil and boil 1 minute. Turn into a large mixing bowl and let cool to lukewarm. Sprinkle yeast into the remaining ½ cup warm water. Let stand until dissolved. Use a vegetable peeler to peel the orange; chop peel coarsely. Place peel in a blender container with 2 tablespoons water and blend until finely chopped. Add yeast, salt, chopped orange peel, butter and molasses to oatmeal mixture. Stir in warm milk; gradually add barley, rye and white flours. Mix to make a soft dough. Turn out on a lightly floured board, knead until smooth and elastic, and place in a large greased bowl. Butter the top lightly and cover with a clean kitchen towel. Let rise until doubled in size, about 1½ hours.

Punch dough down. Knead to remove air bubbles. Divide into 3 parts and shape into loaves. Place in 3 greased 9-x-5-inch loaf pans or shape into round loaves and place on a greased baking sheet. Cover and let rise until doubled in size, about 35 to 40 minutes. Bake in a preheated 375° oven 35 to 40 minutes, or until the loaves sound hollow when thumped.

NUT BREAD

If you have whey available from making yogurt cheese in a net strainer, use it instead of water in this bread for its delightful sour tang. Toasting the walnuts or filberts lends a delicious nutty flavor to this bread. It is ideal sliced and toasted and served with cheese as a special course.

1½ cups walnuts or filberts
1 pkg. active dry yeast
¼ cup warm water
3 tbs. honey
3 tbs. olive oil or nut oil
⅓ cup nonfat dry milk
1½ tsp. salt

1¾ cups warm water or whey from
   making yogurt cheese
2 to 2½ cups unbleached all-
   purpose flour or bread flour
1 cup whole wheat flour
glaze: 1 egg white beaten until
   frothy, optional

Place nuts in a baking dish and toast in a 325° oven for 10 minutes or until light golden. Rub filberts between 2 sheets of paper towels, removing papery skins. Let cool. In a large bowl, sprinkle yeast into warm water and let stand until dissolved and bubbly. Add honey, oil, dry milk, salt and remaining water or whey, mixing well. Add 2 cups unbleached flour and beat until smooth. Add whole wheat flour and remaining unbleached flour, mixing to form a soft dough. Mix in nuts. Knead using a dough hook or by hand. Place in a greased bowl, cover and let rise until doubled, about 1½ hours. Turn out on a floured board and divide in half. Shape into 2 round 8-inch loaves. Place in greased 9-inch baking pans or on a baking sheet. Cover and let rise until doubled. Brush loaves with beaten egg white, if desired. Bake in a preheated 375° oven for 35 minutes or until golden brown.

RUSSIAN BLACK BREAD

Makes 1 loaf

Slices of this rich dark loaf are superb spread with cream cheese topped with lox.

1¾ cups rye flour
1¾ cups unbleached all-purpose
  flour or bread flour
1 tbs. brown sugar
1 tsp. salt
1 cup all-bran cereal
1 tbs. caraway seed, crushed
½ tsp. fennel seed, crushed
1½ tsp. instant coffee powder

1 pkg. active dry yeast
1¼ cups water
2 tbs. cider vinegar
3 tbs. dark molasses
½ oz. (½ square) unsweetened
  chocolate
3 tbs. butter
Cornstarch Glaze

Place ½ cup rye flour, ¾ cup all-purpose flour, brown sugar, salt, cereal, caraway seed, fennel seed, coffee powder and yeast in a large mixing bowl. Stir to blend. Heat water, vinegar, molasses, chocolate and butter together until liquids are very warm (about 125°). Gradually add to dry ingredients. Beat well 2 minutes. Gradually add enough of the remaining rye and bread flours to make a soft dough. Turn out on a lightly floured board and knead until smooth and elastic. Place in a greased bowl, butter top of dough lightly and cover with a clean kitchen towel. Let rise in a warm place until doubled in size, about 1½ hours.

Turn out on a lightly floured board and knead a few times to remove air bubbles. Shape into a round loaf, place in a greased 8-inch round cake pan or on a greased baking sheet, cover and let rise until doubled, about 30 to 40 minutes. Bake in a preheated 350° oven 40 to 45 minutes, or until loaf sounds hollow when thumped. When bread is done, brush top with cornstarch glaze. Bake 2 to 3 minutes longer, or until glaze is set.

Cornstarch Glaze

Bring ¼ cup water to a boil. Blend in 1 tsp. cornstarch which has been mixed with 1 tbs. cold water. Boil, stirring constantly, until thickened.

VARIETY BREAD

Assorted seasonings rolled inside this plain loaf make it extra special.

2 pkg. active dry yeast
2½ cups warm water
1 tbs. sugar
5½ to 6 cups unbleached all-
   purpose flour or bread flour

1 tbs. salt
2 tbs. oil
yellow cornmeal
glaze: 1 egg white beaten with 1 tbs.
   water

Sprinkle yeast into warm water in a mixing bowl. Stir in sugar until dissolved. Gradually beat in 3 cups flour, salt and oil until smooth. Add enough additional flour to make a soft dough. Turn out on a floured board and knead until smooth. Place in a greased bowl, cover with a clean kitchen towel and let rise in a warm place until doubled in size, about 1½ hours.

Punch dough down, turn out on a floured board, and knead several minutes. Divide in half. Shape into two long, French-style loaves. Place on a baking sheet which has been sprinkled with cornmeal. Cover and let rise in a warm place 20 minutes. Slash diagonally with a razor blade, brush with glaze, and bake in a preheated 400° oven 35 to 40 minutes, or until loaves sound hollow when thumped.

Filled Loaves

Let the dough rise once as directed. Punch down, turn out on a lightly floured board and knead a minute or two. Divide in half. Roll each half into a 10-x-14-inch rectangle. Sprinkle surface with one of the suggested fillings, or one of your own choice, shape into loaves and proceed as directed.

Fillings

- ½ cup chopped oil-cured sun-dried tomatoes and 1 tbs. chopped basil
- ½ cup shredded Parmesan cheese and 1 tbs. dried oregano
- ½ cup chopped shallots sautéed in 1 tbs. olive oil
- 4 cloves garlic, roasted and blended with 2 tbs. butter

COUNTRY-STYLE BREAD: FOUGASSE AND FOCACCIA

Makes 2 loaves

Among the more charming breads are fougasse and focaccia, crusty decorative breads of French and Italian origin that can have any flavor variations. This is European country bread at its best — homespun and versatile as it takes on a bevy of seasonings from savory to sweet.

In the south of France, boulangers give their bread made from pain ordinaire a free-form shape by slashing the dough and stretching to resemble a tree of life design or a ladder. This makes a pull-apart loaf known as fougasse that is idea for an informal supper or party occasion.

In Italy, the focaccia has become a staff of life with the crusty dimpled loaves flavored with herbs from the countryside and extra virgin olive oil. The bakers of Italy also combine appealing and creative flavor combinations utilizing prosciutto, sun-dried tomatoes, roasted garlic, caramelized onions, rosemary and thyme, and such cheeses as mozzarella, Gorgonzola, Parmesan and ricotta. These savory styles suit a salad or soup supper. For a sweet version, stud the finger-printed depressions with dried cherries or snipped dried apricots and shower with coarse raw sugar before baking.

36 PLAIN AND WHOLESOME LOAVES

Basic Dough

2 pkg. active dry yeast
½ cup water
pinch sugar or honey
2½ cups water, at room temperature

3 tbs. olive oil
6 cups unbleached all-purpose flour
  or bread flour
2 tsp. salt

Stir yeast into warm water in a large mixing bowl, add sugar and let stand until dissolved and puffy, about 10 minutes. Stir in remaining water and oil. Add 2 cups flour and salt; mix until smooth. Stir in remaining flour, 1 cup at a time. Using a heavy duty mixer, knead with a dough hook about 8 to 10 minutes. Or by hand, knead on a floured surface until smooth and satiny, about 8 to 10 minutes. Place dough in a lightly oiled bowl, cover and let rise until doubled, about 1½ hours. Punch down, turn out on a lightly floured board and knead to eliminate air bubbles. Divide in half.

Fougasse: Roll out each half of the dough into an oblong about 10 x 13 inches and place each piece on a greased baking pan. Use a dough scraper or razor blade to make three diagonal cuts slanting downward on one side of an imaginary center line. Make matching cuts on the other side of the line. Open the cuts by pulling gently. Do not cut through or tear the encircling piece of dough.

Repeat with second pan of dough. Cover with a towel and let rise until doubled.

Focaccia: Divide dough in half and roll out each piece to fit a 10 x 15-inch baking pan. Place in a greased pan and with fingers, dimple dough by making depressions about 1 inch apart. Brush with olive oil. Sprinkle with desired topping: about 2 tsp. coarse sea salt, 1 tsp. chopped rosemary tossed in olive oil or 4 to 6 cloves slightly roasted garlic, chopped. Repeat with second pan of dough. For another topping, stud the surface of the dimpled dough of each focaccia with 6 oz. diced fresh mozzarella cheese, 2 tbs. chopped basil and ½ cup soft oven-dried tomatoes, snipped into pieces. Cover with a towel and let rise until doubled.

For both: Preheat oven to 425°. Place baking pans in the middle of oven and reduce heat to 400°. Bake for 20 to 25 minutes or until golden brown.

BRIOCHE AND EGG BREADS

BRIOCHE 40

BRIOCHE BRAID 41

BRIOCHE CHEESE BRAID . . 42

BRIOCHE WITH CHOCOLATE
  SAUCE 45

BRIOCHE FILBERT ROUNDS . 43

BRIOCHE MOUSSELINE . . . 44

BRIOCHE RING 46

BRIOCHE SANDWICH STAR . 48

CHEESE IN BRIOCHE . . . 42

DESSERT BRIOCHE WITH FRUIT 47

DILL BATTER BREAD . . . 56

FINNISH CELEBRATION BREAD 58

ITALIAN PARMESAN BREAD . 52

MONKEY BREAD 50

ONION SANDWICHES . . . 44

SALLY LUNN 57

SAUSAGE IN BRIOCHE . . . 42

SWISS CINNAMON BRAID . . 60

TURKISH CHEESE BREAD . . 54

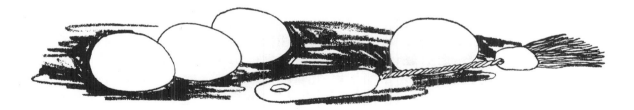

BRIOCHE

Makes 1 large loaf

Buttery egg breads are best served hot to release their flavor and make each morsel meltingly tender. This basic brioche recipe can be used many ways, as you will see.

1 pkg. active dry yeast
¼ cup warm water
½ cup milk
½ cup butter
2 tbs. sugar
½ tsp. salt

3 eggs
1 egg yolk
3¼ cups unbleached all-purpose
   flour or bread flour
egg glaze: 1 egg yolk beaten with 1
   tbs. milk

Sprinkle yeast into warm water and stir until dissolved. Heat milk until warm. In a large bowl, beat butter until creamy. Add sugar, salt, whole eggs and egg yolk. Beat well. Add milk and yeast mixture. Gradually add just enough flour to make a soft dough. Beat well after each addition. Turn out on a lightly floured board, knead until smooth and satiny and place in a greased bowl. Butter top of dough lightly, cover with a clean kitchen towel and let rise in a warm place until doubled in size.

Turn out on a lightly floured board and knead lightly. Cut off ⅕ of the dough for the top-knot. Shape remaining dough into a ball. Place in a greased 2-quart brioche pan. Cut an X in the center with scissors or a sharp knife. Shape reserved dough into a teardrop. Place point down in the X. Cover and let rise until doubled in size. Brush with egg glaze and bake in a preheated 375° oven 30 to 35 minutes, or until the loaf sounds hollow when thumped. Serve warm.

BRIOCHE BRAID
Makes 1 large braid

Prepare brioche dough as directed on page 40. Let rise in a warm place until doubled, about 1½ hours. Turn out on a floured board and knead lightly. Divide dough into 3 pieces. Roll into ropes about 14 inches long. Braid on a greased baking sheet, cover with a kitchen towel and let rise until doubled, about 35 to 40 minutes. Brush with egg glaze, sprinkle with poppy or sesame seeds and bake in a preheated 350° oven 30 to 35 minutes, or until golden brown.

BRIOCHE CHEESE BRAID
Makes 1 large braid

Prepare brioche dough as directed on page 40. Let rise in a warm place until doubled, about 1½ hours. Turn out on a floured board. Knead 1½ cups diced or shredded Jarlsberg or Samsoe cheese into the dough. Divide into 3 pieces and roll into ropes about 14 inches long. Braid dough on a greased baking sheet, cover with a kitchen towel and let rise in a warm place until doubled in size. Bake as directed for *Brioche Braid*.

SAUSAGE IN BRIOCHE   Makes 10-12 entrées or 4-5 dozen appetizers

Prepare brioche dough as directed on page 40. Let dough rise in a warm place until doubled. Punch down. Chill 1 hour or longer for easier handling.

Have cooked sausage ready: simmer 10 to 12 mild Italian sausages (about 3 lbs.) for 20 minutes and chill. Or simmer 2 Italian coteghino sausages (about 3 lbs.) for 40 minutes and chill.

For small sausages, divide the dough into 10 to 12 pieces. For large sausages, divide dough in half. Roll pieces of dough into rectangles about ¼-inch thick. Place a sausage along one side of each rectangle. Roll up, encasing with dough. Place rolls seam side down on a greased baking sheet. Pinch in the ends. Use small aspic cutters to cut out crescents, stars or hearts from dough scraps. Place on top of rolls. Cover with a clean kitchen towel and let rise in a warm place 20 minutes. Brush with egg glaze. Bake in a preheated 375° oven 20 minutes or until nicely browned. Serve as an entrée or slice and serve as appetizers.

CHEESE IN BRIOCHE   Makes 48-60 appetizers

Prepare brioche dough as directed on page 40. Let rise in a warm place until doubled. Punch down. Chill dough 1 hour or longer for easier handling. Divide into 12 pieces, and roll each into a rectangle about ¼-inch thick. Sprinkle each rectangle with ⅓ cup grated Gruyére or Swiss cheese. Roll up like a jelly roll. Decorate the top of each with designs cut from dough scraps. Let stand 10 minutes. Brush with egg glaze and bake in a 375° oven 20 minutes or until browned. Slice and serve hot.

BRIOCHE FILBERT ROUNDS
Makes 2 loaves

Prepare brioche dough as directed on page 40. Let rise in a warm place until doubled, about 1½ hours. Turn out on a floured board. Knead in ½ cup coarsely chopped, toasted filberts. Divide dough in half and shape into balls. Place in 2 well-buttered, tall juice cans (46 oz. size). Cover and let rise in a warm place until doubled. Bake in a preheated 350° oven 35 minutes or until loaves sound hollow when thumped. Remove from cans and cool on racks.

BRIOCHE MOUSSELINE

Here is a richer version of the basic brioche, which is ideal for fancy sandwiches and desserts.

1 pkg. active dry yeast
¼ cup warm water
¼ cup warm milk
1 cup butter

¼ cup sugar
1 tsp. salt
8 eggs
4 cups all-purpose flour

Sprinkle yeast into warm water. Stir until dissolved. In a large bowl, cream butter and beat in sugar, salt and eggs well. Add warm milk and dissolved yeast. Gradually add flour and beat well. This dough will be too soft to knead. Cover with a kitchen towel and let rise until doubled.

Stir down and pour into a greased 10-inch tube pan. Let rise in a warm place until doubled. Bake in a preheated 375° oven 45 minutes.

BRIOCHE ONION SANDWICHES

Cut a *Brioche Mousseline* into thin slices. If desired, cut a 3-inch round from each slice. Blanch 2 sweet red onions in water to cover to 3 minutes. Drain.

Peel and slice very thin. Spread sandwiches with mayonnaise (preferably homemade). Top with onion slices. Dip edges of sandwiches in mayonnaise and then in finely chopped parsley. Cover and chill until serving time.

BRIOCHE WITH CHOCOLATE SAUCE

Cut *Brioche Mousseline* into wedges or rounds. Cover each slice with a spoonful of whipped cream or vanilla ice cream. Top with *Chocolate Sauce* and decorate with whipped cream.

Chocolate Sauce

6 oz. semi-sweet chocolate
1/4 cup light corn syrup

1/2 cup light cream or strong coffee
1 1/2 tbs. brandy or cognac

Heat ingredients together.

BRIOCHE RING

Makes 1 ring

Glaze this lovely bread with apricot preserves and serve with fresh fruit, Cointreau-laced orange sauce and whipped cream.

1 pkg. active dry yeast
1/4 cup warm water
1½ cups unbleached all-purpose
   flour or bread flour

1 tbs. sugar
1 tsp. salt
2 eggs
½ cup soft butter

Sprinkle yeast into warm water and let stand until dissolved. Mix flour, sugar, salt, eggs and dissolved yeast together. Beat until smooth. Beat in butter, 1 tablespoon at a time. Dough will be too soft to knead. Cover and let rise in a warm place until doubled. Punch down and turn into a greased 1½-quart ring mold. Cover and let rise until doubled. Bake in a preheated 375° oven 25 minutes, or until golden brown. Cool slightly on a wire rack before removing from pan.

DESSERT BRIOCHE WITH FRUIT

Bake a *Brioche Ring* as directed. Cool. Bring ½ cup apricot preserves and 1 tablespoon brandy to a boil. Force through a sieve to make a smooth sauce. Brush top of ring with apricot glaze. Place on a serving plate and encircle with apricot halves and bunches of seedless grapes or fresh strawberries. Serve sliced with *Orange Syrup* or pass ice cream balls or whipped cream which has been flavored with kirsch, framboise or Cointreau.

Orange Syrup

½ cup sugar
½ cup water
½ cup orange juice or ¼ cup each Cointreau and brandy

Mix sugar and water together in a small saucepan. Cook until dissolved. Stir in orange juice or Cointreau and brandy.

BRIOCHE SANDWICH STAR

Makes 1 star

This spectacular star-shaped brioche might adorn a party buffet table. It is designed to be filled with assorted finger sandwiches or strips of steak.

1 pkg. active dry yeast
1/4 cup warm water
1/2 cup butter
2 tbs. sugar
1 tsp. salt
1/4 cup brandy, sherry or water

4 eggs
3 1/4 cups unbleached all-purpose
  flour or bread flour
egg glaze: 1 egg yolk beaten with 1
  tbs. milk

Sprinkle yeast into warm water and let stand until dissolved. Cream butter and beat in sugar, salt and brandy, sherry or water. Add eggs one at a time and beat well. Add 1 cup flour and beat well. Stir in dissolved yeast. Gradually add remaining flour, beating well after each addition. Turn out on a floured board and knead until smooth and satiny. Place in a lightly greased bowl, cover with a kitchen towel and let rise in a warm place until doubled, about 1 1/2 hours.

Turn out on a lightly floured board. Knead to release air bubbles. Roll into a 14-inch circle and place on a greased 14-inch pizza pan. With a sharp-pointed knife, cut star points, about 2 1/2 inches long, around the outer edge. Make about 12 to 14 points in all. Shape remaining dough into a ball, roll into a 9-

inch circle and place in the center of the star. Cover and let rise in a warm place until doubled in size. Brush with egg glaze. Bake in a preheated 375° oven for 30 minutes or until golden brown and the loaf sounds hollow when thumped. Let cool on a cake rack.

Filling Suggestions

Assorted sandwiches. With a serrated knife, slice off the center top layer of the *Brioche Star*. Hollow out the middle, removing the bread in one piece. Slice it to make triangular sandwiches, using an assortment of fillings such as smoked salmon, shrimp or crab with cream cheese and watercress; chopped toasted almond or olive and cream cheese; or sliced turkey or ham with chutney. Fit sandwiches back into hollowed center. Replace top layer and serve.

Steak sandwich. Cut top off of *Brioche Star* and cut out the center section. Blend together 2 tbs. soft butter, 1 minced shallot, 2 tsp. minced parsley, ½ tsp. grated lemon peel and 1 clove minced garlic. Spread cut surfaces of hollowed-out center with seasoned butter. Heat loaf in a 350° oven for 10 minutes, or until hot through. Meanwhile, pan fry a 1½ lb. top round or sirloin steak in 1 tbs. butter. Turn to brown both sides; cook medium rare. Remove from pan and slice into very thin strips. Place strips inside of star. Replace top. Cut into pie-shaped wedges to serve. Makes 8 servings.

The *Brioche Star* is illustrated on **Contents** page.

MONKEY BREAD

Serving this bread is great fun. The butter-dipped rolls pull apart with ease from the big handsome ring.

1 pkg. active dry yeast
1/4 cup warm water
1 cup milk
1 cup butter
2 tbs. sugar

3 eggs
1 tsp. salt
4 cups unbleached all-purpose flour
  or bread flour

Sprinkle yeast into warm water. Let stand until dissolved. Heat milk and 1/2 cup butter together until warm. Pour into a mixing bowl, add sugar and eggs and beat until smooth. Stir in dissolved yeast mixture, salt and 1 cup flour. Beat until smooth. Gradually add enough of the remaining flour to make a soft dough. Turn out on a lightly floured board and knead until smooth and satiny. Place in a greased bowl and butter top of dough lightly. Cover with a clean kitchen towel and let rise in a warm place until doubled in size.

Punch dough down. Turn out on a lightly floured board and knead lightly. Melt remaining butter. Roll dough out on a floured board until about 1/3-inch thick.

Using a 2½-inch round cookie cutter or a diamond-shaped cookie cutter, cut dough into rounds or diamonds. Roll and cut scraps until all dough is used. Dip each piece in butter to coat both sides. Place in overlapping layers in a greased 10-inch ring mold (3-quart size). Cover pan with a towel and let rise in a warm place, about 45 minutes. Bake in a preheated 350° oven 35 minutes or until nicely browned and loaf sounds hollow when thumped. Turn out on a large plate and serve warm. Or let cool, wrap air-tight and freeze. Allow to thaw and reheat before serving.

ITALIAN PARMESAN BREAD

Makes 1 round loaf

This mushroom-shaped loaf, streaked with cheese, is a fine companion to an Italian dinner.

1 pkg. active dry yeast
¾ cup warm water
2 tbs. sugar
1 tsp. salt
3 cups unbleached all-purpose flour
4 eggs
½ cup soft butter
1 cup freshly grated Parmesan cheese
1 cup shredded Monterey Jack cheese
1 tsp. fresh rosemary, chopped or 1 tsp. dried oregano, optional

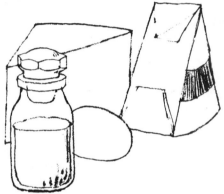

Sprinkle yeast into warm water in a large mixing bowl and let stand until dissolved. Add sugar, salt and 1 cup of flour. Beat well. Add 3 eggs, one at a time, and beat until smooth. Beat in butter. Gradually add enough remaining flour to make a soft dough. Turn out on a floured board and knead until smooth and satiny. Place in a greased bowl and butter top of dough lightly. Cover with a kitchen towel and let rise in a warm place until doubled in size.

Turn out on a floured board and knead lightly. Roll out into a rectangle about 10 x 16 inches. Beat remaining egg. Blend in cheeses and rosemary or oregano. Spread cheese filling over dough. Roll up firmly from narrow end and shape into a round by folding ends underneath. Place in a greased 2-quart round baking dish (preferably one with straight sides about 3 inches high, such as a soufflé dish). Cover and let rise in a warm place until doubled. Bake in a preheated 350° oven 40 minutes, or until golden brown and loaf sounds hollow when thumped. Cool 10 minutes and remove from pan.

TURKISH CHEESE BREAD

Makes 8 pieces

This open-face cheese bread is shaped like an elongated pizza. Serve it hot, sliced in narrow strips for an appetizer or in wider chunks for luncheon.

1 pkg. active dry yeast
¼ cup warm water
6 tbs. soft butter
2 tbs. sugar
3 eggs
½ tsp. salt
½ cup lukewarm milk
3¼ cups unbleached all-purpose flour
Cheese Filling

Sprinkle yeast into warm water and let stand until dissolved. In a large bowl, beat butter and sugar until creamy. Beat in eggs, one at a time. Add salt, milk, dissolved yeast and 1 cup flour. Beat until smooth. Gradually add enough flour to make a soft dough. Turn out on a floured board and knead until smooth. Place in a greased bowl. Cover with a clean kitchen towel and let rise until doubled, about 1½ hours. Turn out on a floured board and knead lightly. Cut into 8 pieces and roll each into a thin rectangle, about 5 x 9 inches. Place on greased baking sheets and spread with *Cheese Filling*. Roll up edges slightly to hold in filling. Let rise 20 minutes. Bake in a preheated 375° oven 25 minutes or until golden brown.

Cheese Filling

½ lb. cream cheese
½ lb. ricotta cheese
⅔ cup grated Parmesan cheese

3 eggs
¼ cup chopped parsley
3 green onions, chopped

Beat ingredients together.

DILL BATTER BREAD

Fragrant dill seeds add crunch to this cheese-streaked round loaf.

1 pkg. active dry yeast
3 cups unbleached all-purpose flour
2 tbs. sugar
2 tbs. dill seed
1 tsp. salt

1¼ cups very warm water (125°)
⅓ cup softened butter
2 eggs
1 cup (4 oz.) shredded cheddar or
  Monterey Jack cheese

Place yeast, 1 cup flour, sugar, dill seed and salt in a large mixing bowl. Pour in water and beat until smooth. Add butter and eggs and beat until blended. Gradually add remaining flour and beat well. Mix in cheese. Cover and let rise in a warm place until doubled.

Stir down. Turn into a greased 2-quart soufflé dish or casserole. Cover and let rise until doubled, about 45 minutes. Bake in a preheated 350° oven 1 hour or until loaf sounds hollow when thumped.

SALLY LUNN

This renowned Southern bread looks festive baked in a fluted tube pan.

1 pkg. active dry yeast
½ cup warm water
1 cup warm milk
½ cup soft butter
¼ cup sugar

1½ tsp. salt
4½ to 5 cups unbleached all-
   purpose or bread flour
3 eggs

Sprinkle yeast into warm water in a large mixing bowl. Let stand until dissolved. Add milk, butter, sugar, salt and 1 cup of flour. Beat until smooth. Add eggs one at a time. Beat well after each addition. Gradually add enough remaining flour to make a soft dough, which is too soft to knead. Place in a greased bowl, cover with a kitchen towel and let rise until doubled in size, about 1½ hours.

Stir dough down. Spoon into a greased 10-inch tube pan or kugelhopf mold. Cover and let rise until doubled, about 45 minutes. Bake in a preheated 375° oven 35 to 40 minutes, or until loaf sounds hollow when thumped.

FINNISH CELEBRATION BREAD

Makes 1 large loaf

This fruit- and nut-filled sweet bread is traditionally baked in a milking pail to celebrate the birth of spring calves.

2 pkg. active dry yeast
½ cup warm water
¾ cup butter
¾ cup sugar
4 eggs
1 tsp. salt
½ tsp. nutmeg
2 tsp. grated lemon peel
1¾ cups lukewarm milk
7 to 8 cups unbleached all-purpose flour
¾ cup chopped filberts or walnuts

Stir yeast into water and let stand until dissolved. In a large bowl, cream butter and sugar. Beat in eggs, salt, nutmeg, lemon peel and milk. Stir in dissolved yeast. Gradually add 4 cups flour and beat well for 5 minutes. Gradually beat in enough remaining flour to make a soft dough. Turn out on a floured board and knead until satiny. Place in a greased bowl and butter top of dough lightly. Cover and let rise in a warm place until almost doubled.

Turn out on a floured board and knead lightly. Shape into a round ball. Place in a greased 4-quart baking dish. Butter top of dough lightly, cover and let rise in a warm place until almost doubled. Bake in a preheated 350° oven 1 hour or until golden brown and bread sounds hollow when thumped. Cool on a wire rack before removing from pan.

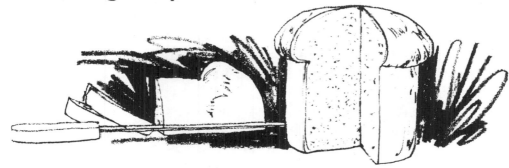

SWISS CINNAMON BRAID

Makes 1 large braid

This spicy-sweet bread is ideal for breakfast or a coffee treat.

1 pkg. active dry yeast
¼ cup warm water
½ cup milk
¼ cup butter
2 tbs. sugar

1 tsp. salt
2 eggs
3 cups unbleached all-purpose flour
cinnamon-sugar: ¼ cup sugar
   blended with 1½ tsp. cinnamon

Sprinkle yeast into warm water and stir until dissolved. Heat milk and butter until butter melts. Pour into a large mixing bowl; add sugar and salt. Cool to lukewarm. Stir in yeast mixture and beat in eggs, one at a time. Gradually beat in enough flour to make a soft dough. Turn out on a floured board and knead until smooth and satiny. Place in a greased bowl and butter top of dough lightly. Cover with a kitchen towel and let rise in warm place until doubled, about 1½ hours.

Turn out on a floured board and knead lightly. Cut into 3 pieces. Roll each piece between the palms of your hands, making strips about 10 inches long. Roll strips in cinnamon-sugar. Place sugared strips on a buttered baking sheet and braid. Tuck ends under braid. Cover and let rise in a warm place until doubled in size. Bake in a preheated 350° oven 30 to 35 minutes, or until golden brown. Cool on a wire rack.

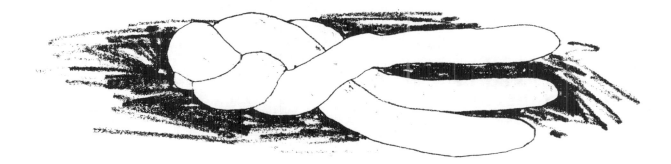

SPECIALTY ROLLS

DINNER ROLLS 63
HOLLAND BRIOCHE CAKES . 66
HOT CROSS BUNS 68
LEBANESE ANISE BUNS. . . 70
CARAMEL CINNAMON TWISTS 72
FILBERT CRESCENTS . . . 74
CARAMEL PECAN ROLLS . . 76
FROSTED PINWHEELS . . . 78
CINNAMON ROLLS 79

DANISH PASTRY COCKSCOMBS 80
CROISSANTS 82
FRENCH-STYLE CRUSTY ROLLS 84
PITA 86
ONION BUNS 88
SESAME HAMBURGER BUNS . 90
MEXICAN PAN DULCE . . . 92
ITALIAN SALT STICKS . . . 95
SWEDISH ALMOND CRESCENTS 96

DINNER ROLLS

Make tender dinner rolls in any of a number of different shapes to grace your table and please your guests.

2 pkg. active dry yeast
½ cup warm water
1 cup milk
½ cup butter
2 tbs. sugar

1 tsp. salt
1 tsp. vanilla or grated lemon peel
3 eggs
5 cups unbleached all-purpose flour
1 egg white, lightly beaten

Sprinkle yeast into warm water and let stand until dissolved. Heat milk and butter together until butter melts. Pour into a large mixing bowl and stir in sugar, salt and vanilla or lemon peel. Cool to lukewarm and stir in dissolved yeast. Add eggs one at a time and beat until smooth. Gradually beat in enough flour to make a soft dough. Turn out on a floured board and knead until smooth and satiny. Place in a greased bowl, butter top of dough lightly, cover and let rise in a warm place until doubled, about 1½ hours.

Punch down. Turn out on a floured board and shape in any of the following ways. Cover with a towel and let rise until doubled. Bake in a preheated 375°

oven 15 minutes or until golden brown.

SHAPING DINNER ROLLS

Bowknots: Roll dough about ½-inch thick. Cut into 9-inch long strips. Tie in loose knots and tuck ends under. Place on greased baking sheets and cover for second rise.

Cloverleaf rolls: Shape dough into small balls about ¾-inch in diameter. Place 3 balls in each greased muffin cup and cover for second rise.

Crescents: Roll dough into 12-inch circles, ¼-inch thick. Brush with melted butter. Cut into 8 to 12 wedges. Starting at the wide side, roll up each wedge and shape rolls into crescents. Place on greased baking sheets and cover for second rise.

Parker House rolls: Roll dough ½-inch thick. Cut with a 3- to 4-inch round cutter. Brush with melted butter, fold in half and press edges to seal. Place on greased baking sheets and cover for second rise.

Rosettes: Roll dough about ½-inch thick and cut into 12-inch strips. Form into a loose knot, leaving two long ends. Tuck top end under roll. Bring bottom end up and tuck into center of roll. Place on greased baking sheets and cover for second rise.

Corkscrews: Roll dough about ½-inch thick. Cut into 8-inch-long strands. Wrap each one around a greased wooden clothespin. Place on greased baking sheets and cover for second rise. Remove clothespins after baking.

Braids: Form dough into several ropes about ½ inch in diameter. Braid 3 ropes at a time into a long braid. Cut into 3½-inch lengths. Pinch together at each end and pull braid slightly to lengthen. Place on greased baking sheets and cover for second rise.

HOLLAND BRIOCHE CAKES

Makes 2 dozen

These aromatic lemon buns are delightful for brunch. If you intend to freeze some, wait and frost those later.

1 pkg. active dry yeast
¼ cup warm water
¾ cup milk
⅓ cup sugar
⅓ cup butter
1 tsp. salt
2 eggs
1 tsp. grated lemon peel
1 tbs. lemon juice
3½ cups unbleached all-purpose flour
melted butter

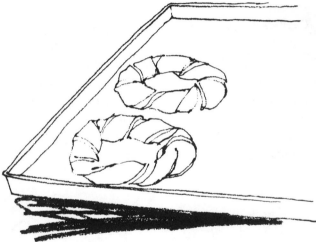

Sprinkle yeast into warm water and let stand until dissolved. Heat milk and pour over sugar, butter and salt in a large mixing bowl. Let cool to lukewarm. Add dissolved yeast, eggs, lemon peel and juice. Beat until smooth. Gradually add half of the flour and beat 2 minutes. Stir in remaining flour and beat well. Turn out on a floured board. Knead until smooth and satiny. Place in a greased bowl, cover with a kitchen towel and let rise until doubled in size, about 1½ hours.

Turn out on a floured board and knead lightly. Roll out to about - inch thick. Brush with melted butter and fold over in thirds. The total width of the dough should be 9 inches. With a sharp knife, cut into ½-inch strips. Twist, form a loop, and tuck ends underneath. Place on greased baking sheets. Cover and let rise until doubled. Bake in a preheated 375° oven 15 to 20 minutes, or until golden brown. Cool on a rack. Spread with *Orange Frosting*.

Orange Frosting
1 cup powdered sugar
1 tbs. orange juice

Blend ingredients.

HOT CROSS BUNS

Makes 2 dozen

Spicy hot cross buns have been an English tradition for centuries. Originally they were passed out to holiday travelers.

1 pkg. active dry yeast
4 cups unbleached all-purpose flour
⅓ cup sugar
½ tsp. salt
¾ tsp. cinnamon
¼ tsp. nutmeg

1 cup milk
¼ cup butter
2 eggs
½ cup currants
¼ cup diced citron, optional
Lemon Glaze

Combine yeast, 1 cup flour, sugar, salt, cinnamon and nutmeg in a mixing bowl. Heat milk and butter to about 125°, pour over dry ingredients and beat until smooth. Beat in eggs, one at a time. Gradually add remaining flour, beating well. Mix in currants and citron. Turn out on a floured board and knead until smooth and satiny. Place in a greased bowl and butter top lightly. Cover and let rise in a warm place until almost doubled.

Turn dough out on a floured board and knead lightly. Cut off pieces about the size of a golf ball. Roll between the palms of your hands. Place on a lightly greased baking sheet, cover and let rise until almost doubled in size. With a razor blade or sharp knife, cut a cross in the surface of each bun. Bake in a preheated 375° oven 15 to 20 minutes, or until golden brown. Let cool on a wire rack. Drizzle *Lemon Glaze* over tops of buns in a cross design.

Lemon Glaze
1 cup powdered sugar   1½ tbs. milk
1 tsp. grated lemon peel

Blend ingredients.

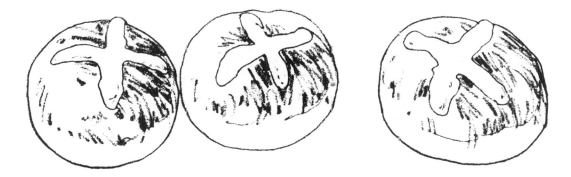

LEBANESE ANISE BUNS (KA'ICK)

Makes 2 dozen

These anise-flavored buns are coated with delicious sweet syrup.

1 pkg. active dry yeast
3 cups unbleached all-purpose flour
½ cup sugar
1 tsp. anise seed
½ tsp. salt

¾ cup milk
½ cup butter
1 egg
Orange Flower Syrup

Combine yeast, 1 cup flour, sugar, anise seed and salt in a mixing bowl. Heat milk and butter to about 125°. Pour mixture over dry ingredients and beat until smooth. Beat in egg. Gradually add enough remaining flour to make a soft dough. Turn out on a lightly floured board and knead until smooth and satiny. Place in a greased bowl and butter top of dough lightly. Cover and let rise in a warm place until almost doubled in size.

Turn dough out on a floured board and knead lightly. Cut into small pieces, about 2 inches in diameter. Cover with a towel and let rest 10 minutes. On a lightly floured board, roll into discs about 3½ inches in diameter and ¼ inch thick. Place on a lightly greased baking sheet and let rise in a warm place until almost doubled. Bake in a preheated 350° oven 15 to 20 minutes, or until golden brown. Let cool on wire racks. Using a fork, dip breads one at a time into hot syrup, coating completely. Place on a serving tray to cool.

Orange Flower Syrup

½ cup sugar
¼ cup milk
2 tbs. butter

1 tsp. orange flower water or rose water

Combine ingredients in a saucepan, bring to a boil and boil 2 minutes.

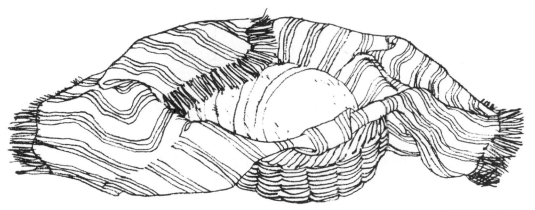

CARAMEL CINNAMON TWISTS

Makes 4 dozen

Caramelized cinnamon-sugar gilds these spiral rolls with crunchy candy.

1 cup butter, melted
1 cup sour cream
1 tsp. salt
1 tsp. vanilla
1 pkg. active dry yeast
2 egg yolks
1 egg
3½ cups unbleached all-purpose flour
1½ cups sugar
2 tsp. cinnamon

Mix together hot butter, sour cream, salt and vanilla. The mixture should be lukewarm. Sprinkle in yeast. Beat egg yolks and egg until blended and stir into yeast mixture. Stir in enough flour to make a soft dough and beat until smooth. It is not necessary to knead this dough. Cover bowl with plastic wrap and chill 2 hours.

Mix sugar and cinnamon and spread half of it on a board. Divide dough in half. Roll each piece of dough into a rectangle (15 x 18 inches). Turn dough in the cinnamon-sugar mixture so both sides are coated. Fold over 3 times, as you would fold a letter. Repeat rolling, coating and folding 3 times until sugar mixture is almost used. Roll into a rectangle 1/4-inch thick. Cut into strips 1/2-inch wide by 4 inches long. Twist strips. Dip in remaining cinnamon-sugar mixture. Lay on a greased baking sheet. Repeat with remaining dough and sugar mixture. Cover with a towel and let rise in a warm place until light and puffy. Bake in a preheated 375° oven 15 minutes, or until golden brown. Serve hot or reheat.

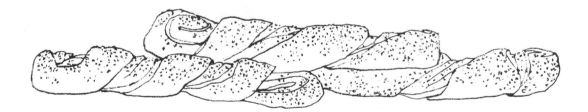

FILBERT CRESCENTS

A delectable filbert paste swirls within these tender refrigerator crescents.

1 pkg. active dry yeast
¼ cup warm water
½ cup butter
3 cups unbleached all-purpose flour
⅓ cup light cream or milk
¼ cup sugar
½ tsp. ground cardamom
3 eggs
Nut Filling
1 egg white
½ cup chopped filberts
sugar

Sprinkle yeast into warm water and let stand until dissolved. Cut butter into flour until mixture resembles oatmeal. Heat cream or milk until lukewarm and pour into a large mixing bowl. Add sugar and cardamom. Stir in dissolved yeast and 1 cup butter-flour mixture. Beat until smooth. Beat in eggs, one at a time. Add remaining butter-flour mixture and beat until smooth. It is not necessary to knead this dough. Cover with plastic wrap or foil and chill several hours or overnight.

Divide chilled dough into 4 equal pieces. Roll out each piece on a lightly floured board into a circle about 15 inches in diameter. Spread ¼ of the nut filling over each circle of dough. Cut each circle into 8 pie-shaped wedges. Roll wedges up starting at large end. Place on greased baking sheets with points underneath. Curve rolls to form crescents, cover with a towel and let rise in a warm place until doubled. Beat egg white lightly and brush over top of crescents. Sprinkle with filberts and sugar. Bake in a preheated 350° oven 20 minutes, or until golden brown.

Nut Filling

1 cup filberts or blanched almonds   1 egg
½ cup sugar   ⅓ cup soft butter

Combine nuts, sugar and egg in a blender and blend until smooth. Stir mixture into butter.

CARAMEL PECAN ROLLS

Children adore these wonderful chewy, sticky rolls.

2 pkg. active dry yeast
1/2 cup warm water
1 cup milk
1/2 cup butter
2/3 cup sugar
1 tsp. salt
1 tsp. vanilla

3 eggs
5 cups unbleached all-purpose flour
melted butter
cinnamon
1 cup light brown sugar
Caramel Pecan Coating

Sprinkle yeast into warm water and let stand until dissolved. Heat milk and butter together until butter melts. Pour into a large mixing bowl and stir in sugar, salt and vanilla. Cook to lukewarm and stir in yeast mixture. Add eggs one at a time and beat until smooth. Gradually beat in enough flour to make a soft dough. Turn out on a floured board and knead until smooth and satiny. Place in a greased bowl and butter top of dough lightly. Cover with a kitchen towel and let rise until doubled in size, about 1 1/2 hours.

Divide dough in half and knead lightly. Roll each piece into a 10-x-12-inch rectangle. Spread with melted butter and sprinkle lightly with cinnamon. Scatter

½ cup brown sugar onto each rectangle. Roll up and cut into ¾-inch slices. Place in prepared caramel-coated pans, cover and let rise until doubled in size. Bake in a preheated 350° oven 30 minutes, or until golden brown. Immediately turn upside down on racks and lift off pans. Serve warm or cool.

Caramel Pecan Coating

Select three 9-inch-square baking pans. Place 2½ tbs. butter, ¼ cup light corn syrup and ⅔ cup firmly packed light brown sugar in each pan. Heat in a 350° oven just until butter melts and mixture bubbles. Spread coating evenly over bottom of pans. Scatter ⅓ cup pecan halves onto each caramel-coated pan. Top with sliced dough as directed.

FROSTED PINWHEELS

Makes 3 dozen

Orange frosting glazes raisin-studded pinwheels.

2 pkg. active dry yeast
½ cup warm water
1 cup milk
¾ cup butter
⅓ cup sugar
½ tsp. salt

½ tsp. almond extract
6 eggs
6½ cups unbleached all-purpose
 flour
Raisin Filling
Orange Frosting

Sprinkle yeast into warm water and let stand until dissolved. Heat milk to lukewarm. In a large bowl, cream butter and sugar. Beat in salt, almond extract and eggs. Stir in dissolved yeast and milk. Gradually add enough flour to make a soft dough. Turn out on a floured board and knead until smooth and satiny. Place in a greased bowl, cover with a kitchen towel and let rise in a warm place until doubled.

Punch dough down. Turn out on a floured board and knead lightly. Roll out into a large rectangle about ⅓-inch thick. Spread with *Raisin Filling,* roll up and cut into ½-inch thick slices. Place on greased baking sheets 2 inches apart, cover and let rise in a warm place until doubled, about 45 minutes. Bake in a preheated 375° oven 20 to 25 minutes or until golden brown. Cool slightly and spread with *Orange Frosting*.

Raisin Filling

¾ cup brown sugar   3 tbs. melted butter
½ cup raisins   1 tbs. cinnamon

Mix ingredients together.

Orange Frosting

2 cups powdered sugar   2 tbs. water
2 tbs. orange juice concentrate

Mix ingredients together.

Cinnamon Rolls

Follow directions for *Frosted Pinwheels*, except place 12 slices in each of 3 greased 9-x-1½-inch-round cake pans. Cover and let rise in a warm place until doubled in size, about 30 minutes. Bake in a preheated 375° oven about 20 to 25 minutes. Drizzle vanilla frosting or *Orange Frosting* over warm rolls.

DANISH PASTRY COCKSCOMBS

Hear are bear claws, an all-time favorite.

1 pkg. active dry yeast
½ cup lukewarm water
5 cups unbleached all-purpose flour
1½ cups butter
2 eggs
1 egg yolk
1 cup milk, heated to lukewarm

3 tbs. sugar
1 tsp. salt
1 tsp. ground cardamom
Almond Cream Filling
1 egg white, lightly beaten
coarse granulated sugar

Sprinkle yeast into lukewarm water and let stand until dissolved. Measure 4 cups flour into a mixing bowl. Cut in ½ cup butter until the size of peas. Add eggs, egg yolk, milk, yeast, sugar, salt and cardamom. Mix until blended. Gradually stir in remaining flour. Turn dough out onto a floured board and knead until light. Roll into a rectangle ½-inch thick, 12 inches wide and 18 inches long. Cut remaining butter into thin slices. Place half of it on the center third of the rectangle. Fold over 1 side. Place remaining butter on top and fold over remaining side. Roll out ½-inch thick and fold in thirds. Place on a baking pan and cover with plastic wrap. Chill 15 minutes. Repeat rolling, folding and chilling steps 3 times. Dough is then ready for shaping.

Roll out into a long strip. Cut in 6 strips, each 3 to 4 inches wide. Roll each strip ⅛-inch thick, 5 inches wide and 21 inches long. Mark off into thirds, lengthwise. Spread a band of filling down the center third. Fold one side of dough over the center. Fold remaining third on top. Flip over, seam side down, and cut crosswise in 3-inch wide pieces. Make 3 deep gashes in each piece along one folded edge. Place on a buttered baking sheet and let rise until doubled, about 1 hour. Brush with slightly beaten egg white and sprinkle with sugar. Bake in a preheated 375° oven 15 to 20 minutes, or until golden brown.

Almond Cream Filling

¼ cup butter
1 cup powdered sugar
2 egg yolks

2 tbs. rum
1 cup ground almonds

Beat ingredients together.

CROISSANTS

Flakiness is achieved by cutting butter into the flour as when making pastry. Butter nuggets melt as the rolls bake, making many paper-thin layers.

1 pkg. active dry yeast
1/4 cup warm water
2 egg yolks
1 cup lukewarm milk
1 tbs. sugar

1/2 tsp. salt
3 1/2 cups unbleached all-purpose
  flour
1 cup butter
1 egg white, beaten until frothy

Sprinkle yeast into warm water and let stand until dissolved. Beat egg yolks; stir in warm milk, sugar, salt, yeast mixture and 2/3 cup flour. Beat until smooth and set aside. In another bowl, cut butter into remaining flour until particles are the size of large peas. Pour in yeast mixture. Mix lightly with a spatula just until flour is moistened. Cover bowl with plastic wrap and chill at least 2 hours or until cold. (If desired, chill up to 3 days.)

Turn out on a floured board and knead lightly. Divide into thirds. Roll each piece of dough into a circle about 16 inches in diameter. Cut into 12 pie-shaped wedges. For each croissant, roll wedges starting at the outer edge of the circle. Place rolls point down on a greased baking sheet, cover with a towel and let rise at room temperature until doubled. Brush surface with beaten egg white. Bake in a preheated 375° oven 20 minutes or until golden brown. Serve warm.

FRENCH-STYLE CRUSTY ROLLS

Makes 18 rolls

A remarkably crisp crust distinguishes these round white buns. They freeze and reheat beautifully, retaining their crunch.

1 pkg. active dry yeast
1½ cups warm water
3¼ cups unbleached all-purpose
  flour

1½ tsp. salt
cornmeal
egg white glaze: 1 egg white lightly
  beaten with 1 tsp. water

Sprinkle yeast into warm water in a large mixing bowl. Let stand until dissolved. Gradually add flour and salt, beating until smooth. Turn dough out on a lightly floured board and knead until smooth. Place in a greased bowl and butter top of dough lightly. Cover with a clean kitchen towel and let rise in a warm place until doubled, about 1½ hours.

Punch down, cover with a towel and let rise again until doubled. Turn out on a floured board and knead lightly. Cut into 18 equal pieces. Shape each piece into a round ball and place on a greased baking sheet that is lightly sprinkled with cornmeal. Brush with egg white glaze and place in a warm place to rise. Make a tent with a tightly wrung-out, wet kitchen towel to cover the rolls as they rise. This is important, as it helps make the crust crisp. To prepare the oven for baking the rolls, place a pan of hot water on the lower rack and preheat oven to 375°. When rolls have doubled, brush again with glaze and bake on the rack above the steaming water 15 minutes. Brush again with glaze and bake 15 minutes longer, or until golden brown.

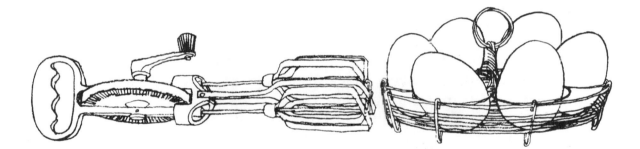

PITA (ARABIC, MEDITERRANEAN, OR POCKET BREAD) Makes 12

Various names identify this saucer-like bread. Each round puffs up like a balloon during baking, and then collapses, forming a neat inner pocket.

2 cups warm water
1 pkg. active dry yeast
2 tsp. sugar
4½ cups unbleached all-purpose
  flour

1½ tsp. salt
3 tbs. olive oil or vegetable oil

Pour ¼ cup water into a small bowl, add yeast and sugar and stir just to blend. Let stand until dissolved. Place flour, salt and oil in a mixing bowl. Add yeast mixture and remaining 1¾ cups water. Beat until flour is completely moistened. Turn dough out on a floured board and knead until smooth and no longer sticky, about 5 to 10 minutes. Place in a greased bowl and oil top of dough lightly. Cover with a clean kitchen towel and let rise in a warm place until doubled in size, about 1¼ hours.

Turn out on a floured board and knead lightly to remove air bubbles. Roll into a log 12 inches long. Cut into 12 equal pieces. Pat each piece of dough into a ball. Using a rolling pin, roll each ball of dough on a floured board into a 6½-inch round about ¼-inch thick. Place on lightly greased baking sheets and let rise in a warm place, uncovered, until barely doubled in thickness. Move oven rack to lowest slot and preheat oven to 500°. Bake one pan at a time about 5 minutes, or until bread is puffed and just starting to brown. Remove from oven and place on wire racks. Serve while warm or let cool slightly and slip into plastic bags to stay moist and pliable.

If desired, freeze. To serve later, let thaw, stack together and wrap in foil. Reheat in a 375° oven 10 to 15 minutes, or until heated through.

ONION BUNS

Makes 3 dozen

These robust whole wheat buns are excellent for sandwiches.

3 tbs. butter
1 cup finely chopped onion
3 cups unbleached all purpose flour
3 cups whole wheat flour

3 tbs. sugar
2 tsp. salt
2 pkg. active dry yeast
2 cups very warm water (125°)

Melt butter in a frying pan and sauté onion until golden, about 5 to 7 minutes. Set aside. Blend together 1 cup all-purpose flour, 1 cup whole wheat flour, sugar, salt and yeast in a large electric mixer bowl. Reserve 2 tablespoons of onion-butter mixture and add remainder to dry ingredients. Pour in warm water and beat at low speed 2 minutes. Add 1 cup whole wheat flour and beat at high speed 2 minutes. Stir in remaining 1 cup whole wheat flour and enough of the all-purpose flour (about 1 cup) to make a soft dough. Sprinkle about ⅓ cup all-purpose flour on a bread board. Turn dough out on board and knead until smooth and elastic, about 5 minutes. Add more flour as needed. Place in a greased bowl and butter top of dough lightly. Cover and let rise in a warm place until doubled in size.

Punch dough down and divide into 36 golf ball-sized pieces. Shape into buns. Place ½-inch apart on greased baking sheets. Sprinkle ¼ teaspoon reserved onion on the top of each bun. Cover with a towel and let rise in a warm place until doubled. Bake in a preheated 375° oven 20 to 25 minutes or until golden brown.

SESAME HAMBURGER BUNS

Makes 2 dozen

Plump, freshly made hamburger buns are always a big hit at a barbecue. Split and toast them on the grill, if you like.

1 pkg. active dry yeast
¼ cup warm water
½ cup butter
2 tbs. sugar
3 eggs
1 cup milk, room temperature
1 tsp. salt
4 cups unbleached all-purpose flour
1 egg white, lightly beaten
¼ cup sesame seeds

Sprinkle yeast into warm water and let stand until dissolved. In a large bowl, cream butter and sugar; beat in eggs, milk and salt. Add dissolved yeast. Gradually add enough flour to make a soft dough. Turn out onto a lightly floured board and knead until smooth and satiny. Place dough in a greased bowl and butter top lightly. Cover with a clean kitchen towel and let rise in a warm place until doubled in size.

Punch dough down. Turn out on a floured board and knead lightly. Divide into 24 balls. Turn each ball in your hands, folding edges under to make an even circle. Press flat between hands. Place on greased baking sheets and press each to a 3¼-inch circle. Cover with a towel and let rise in a warm place until doubled in size. Brush with lightly beaten egg white and sprinkle with sesame seeds. Bake in a preheated 375° oven 10 to 15 minutes or until golden brown. Cool on a wire rack or serve warm.

MEXICAN PAN DULCE

Makes 14 buns

Top these fanciful Mexican sweet buns with either plain or chocolate streusel and shape them in any of several different ways.

1 cup milk
⅓ cup butter
1 pkg. active dry yeast
1 tsp. salt
⅓ cup sugar
3¼ cups unbleached all-purpose
 flour

2 eggs
Plain Streusel
Chocolate Streusel
egg wash: 1 egg beaten with 2 tbs.
 milk

Place milk and butter in a saucepan and heat until very warm, about 125°. Place yeast, salt, sugar and 1 cup flour in a large mixing bowl. Pour in heated milk mixture and beat until smoothly blended. Add eggs, one at a time, and beat until smooth. Gradually add remaining flour and beat until smooth. Turn out on a floured board and knead 10 minutes, or until satiny and no longer sticky. Place in a greased bowl and butter top of dough lightly. Cover with a clean kitchen towel and let rise in a warm place until doubled in size.

Turn out on a floured board and knead lightly. Cut dough into 14 equal pieces and shape each into a ball. Then finish in a variety of ways, following the directions given on this page and page 94. Complete with streusel, using *Plain Streusel* on half of the buns and *Chocolate Streusel* on the other. Place on a lightly greased baking sheet and let rise until doubled, about 45 minutes. Brush lightly with egg wash. Bake in a 375° oven 20 minutes, or until golden brown.

Plain Streusel

3/4 cup sugar   6 tbs. butter
1 cup flour   3 egg yolks

Blend sugar, flour and butter until crumbly. Blend in egg yolks. Makes enough for 7 buns.

Chocolate Streusel

Prepare *Plain Streusel*, adding 1/4 cup unsweeted cocoa to dry ingredients. Makes enough for 7 buns.

Concho (shell): For each bun, shape dough ball into a 3-inch round, 3/4-inch thick, and place on a greased baking sheet. Take 1/4 cup *Plain* or *Chocolate Streusel* and pat into a ball. Then, on a lightly floured board, roll into a 3-inch round, 1/8-inch thick. Lay streusel on dough, pressing in lightly. With a small sharp knife, score streusel in 4 or 5 arcs to resemble a shell. Or for square-topped style, score streusel in straight lines 3/8-inch apart, and score again in lines 3/8-inch apart, making small squares. Bake as directed.

Picon (coffeecake): Shape dough balls as for Concho. Sprinkle streusel on top of dough, piling it about 1/2-inch thick. Pat it over the entire surface. Bake as directed.

Elote (corn): On a lightly floured surface, roll out each ball of dough about 4 inches wide and 8 inches long. Sprinkle entire surface with 2 tbs. streusel. Roll up, pulling the ends slightly to stretch them. Place on a greased baking sheet and score surface with crosswise slashes 1/4-inch apart. Bake as directed.

Cuerno mantequilla (butterhorn): On a floured surface, roll out each ball of dough about 4 inches wide and 8 inches long. Sprinkle entire surface with 2 tbs. streusel. Roll in the long sides, tapering to a point. Take the long end, and pulling it gently, roll up, making a crescent. Place on a greased baking sheet. Bake as directed.

ITALIAN SALT STICKS

Makes 20 sticks

These delicious bread sticks are a perfect accompaniment to a bowl of hot soup or a luncheon salad.

3 cups unbleached all-purpose flour
1 tbs. sugar
1 tsp. salt
1 pkg. active dry yeast
1/4 cup olive oil or vegetable oil

1 1/4 cups very warm water (125°)
egg white glaze: 1 egg white lightly
  beaten with 1 tbs. water
coarse salt

Place 1 cup flour, sugar, salt and yeast in a large electric mixer bowl. Add oil. Gradually stir in water and beat at medium speed 2 minutes. Add 1/2 cup flour and beat at high speed 2 minutes. Add enough remaining flour to make a soft dough. Turn out on a well-floured board and knead several minutes. Work dough into a smooth ball and shape into a log. Cut into 20 equal-sized pieces. Roll each piece into a rope about 16 inches long. Or make small ropes 6 to 8 inches long. Arrange 1 inch apart on oiled baking sheets. Roll to spread oil on all sides of dough. Cover and let rise in a warm place until puffy, about 15 minutes. Paint each stick with egg white glaze and sprinkle with coarse salt. Bake in a preheated 325° oven 25 to 30 minutes or until browned.

SWEDISH ALMOND CRESCENTS

Almond paste ribbons through these decorative Scandinavian coffee cakes for a superb brunch treat. The rolls are cleverly shaped by cutting wheels of dough into wedges and rolling them with filling.

½ cup butter
3 cups unbleached all-purpose flour
1 pkg. active dry yeast
¼ cup warm water
⅓ cup milk
¼ cup sugar

3 eggs
Almond Paste Filling
1 egg white
1 tbs. water
½ cup sliced almonds
sugar

Cut butter into flour until it resembles oatmeal. Sprinkle yeast into warm water and let stand until dissolved. Scald milk; pour into a large mixing bowl, add sugar, and let cool to lukewarm. Add yeast mixture and 1 cup of flour mixture; beat until smooth. Beat in eggs, one at a time, and the remaining flour mixture, beating until smooth. Cover with plastic wrap and chill overnight.

Divide chilled dough into 4 equal pieces. On a lightly floured board, roll each piece into a circle about 15 inches in diameter. Spread ¼ of the almond filling over each circle. Cut each circle into 8 pie-shaped wedges and roll up. Place on greased baking sheets with points underneath and curve to form crescents. Cover and let rise in a warm place until doubled, about 40 minutes. Beat egg white and water together and brush over top. Sprinkle with almonds and sugar. Bake in a preheated 350° oven for 20 minutes, or until golden brown.

Almond Paste Filling

1 can (8 oz.) almond paste
1/4 cup soft butter

1/3 cup sugar
1 egg

Beat ingredients together until smooth.

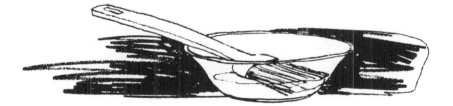

INTERNATIONAL HOLIDAY BREADS

BUCCELLATI	99
PANETTONE	100
PORTUGUESE SWEET BREAD	102
KULICH	104
CHOCOLATE STREUSEL EASTER BREAD	106
ORNAMENTAL WREATH	109
DANISH KRINGLER	110
DRESDEN STOLLEN	112
HONEY NUT STOLLEN	114
GREEK EASTER BREAD	116
GREEK EASTER TWISTS	117
DANISH COFFEE TWIST	119
ITALIAN EASTER DOVE	122
JEWISH CHALLAH	124
RUSSIAN KRENDL	126
GREEK CHRISTMAS BREAD	128
VIENNESE EASTER TWIST	130
CZECHOSLOVAKIAN VANOCKA	132
PUEBLO FESTIVAL BREAD	134

BUCCELLATI

Makes 3 rings

Northern Italy contributes this wine-scented, ring-shaped bread.

1 pkg. active dry yeast
1/4 cup warm water
1/2 cup butter
1/2 cup sugar
4 eggs
1 cup lukewarm milk

2 tsp. anise seed
1 tsp. grated lemon peel
2 tbs. Marsala or port
1/2 tsp. salt
5 cups unbleached all-purpose flour
1 egg white, slightly beaten

Sprinkle yeast into warm water and let stand until dissolved. Cream butter. Beat in sugar and eggs, one at a time. Mix in milk, anise seed, lemon peel, Marsala and salt. Add 1 cup flour and beat until smooth. Stir in dissolved yeast. Gradually add enough remaining flour to make a soft dough. Turn out on a lightly floured board and knead until smooth and satiny. Place in a greased bowl, cover and let rise until doubled in size.

Turn out on a lightly floured board and knead a few minutes. Cut into 3 pieces and shape each into a round cake. Make a hole in the center of each cake and stretch out, making a skinny loop about 8 inches in diameter. Place the rings on greased baking sheets, cover, and let rise until doubled. Bake in a preheated 375° oven 25 to 30 minutes or until golden brown.

PANETTONE

Makes 2 loaves

Chewy raisins and nuts jewel this sweet brioche-style Italian bread.

¾ cup milk
1 pkg. active dry yeast
¼ cup lukewarm water
½ cup butter
½ cup sugar
3 eggs
3½ cups unbleached all-purpose flour
1 tsp. vanilla
1 tsp. grated lemon peel
½ tsp. cinnamon
½ cup golden raisins, plumped in brandy or dry sherry
½ cup dark raisins, plumped in brandy or dry sherry
½ cup slivered almonds or pine nuts
1 egg white, lightly beaten

Heat milk until warm. Sprinkle yeast into warm water and let stand until dissolved. Beat butter until creamy and beat in sugar. Add eggs one at a time and beat until smooth. Add 1 cup flour and beat well. Stir in yeast, milk, vanilla, lemon peel and cinnamon. Gradually add remaining flour and beat until smooth. Mix in raisins and almonds. Turn out on a lightly floured board and knead until smooth and no longer sticky. Place in a greased bowl and butter top of dough lightly. Cover with a clean kitchen towel and let rise in a warm place until doubled in size.

Turn out on a floured board and knead lightly. Divide in half. Shape into 2 round cakes about 6 inches in diameter. Place on a greased baking sheet or in greased cake pans, cover, and let rise until doubled. Bake in a preheated 350° oven 30 minutes, or until golden brown. Let cool on a wire rack. Slice and serve warm or at room temperature.

PORTUGUESE SWEET BREAD

Makes 1 loaf

During baking, this citrus-scented loaf forms a crackly sugar crust.

1 pkg. active dry yeast
¼ cup warm water
½ cup milk
¼ cup butter
½ cup sugar
½ tsp. salt

2 eggs
2 tsp. grated lemon peel
3½ cups unbleached all-purpose
  flour
egg glaze: 1 egg yolk beaten with 1
  tbs. milk

Sprinkle yeast into warm water and let stand until dissolved. Heat milk and butter until butter melts. Pour into a mixing bowl containing sugar and salt; let cool to lukewarm. Add eggs one at a time. Stir in lemon peel and yeast mixture. Gradually beat in flour, adding enough to make a soft dough. Turn out on a lightly floured board and knead until smooth and satiny. Place in a greased bowl and butter top of dough lightly. Cover with a kitchen towel and let rise in a warm place until doubled in size.

Turn out on a lightly floured board and knead gently. Shape into a flat cake about 9 inches in diameter. Place in a greased 9-inch springform pan with removable bottom, or on a greased baking sheet. Cover with a towel and let rise in a warm place until doubled in size. Brush with egg glaze. Bake in a preheated 325° oven 35 to 40 minutes or until golden brown. Let cool on a wire rack; then remove from pan. Slice and serve warm with sweet butter.

KULICH

This Russian Easter bread bakes in a 2-pound coffee can to achieve its stately height. It is traditional to lay a single rosebud on top of the frosting glaze.

1 pkg. active dry yeast
2½ cups unbleached all-purpose flour
¼ cup sugar
½ tsp. salt
½ cup milk
6 tbs. butter
1 egg
2 egg yolks
1 tsp. grated lemon peel
¼ cup golden raisins
¼ cup dark raisins
2 tbs. sherry
¼ cup chopped blanched almonds
Powdered Sugar Glaze: ½ cup powdered sugar blended with 1½ tsp. milk

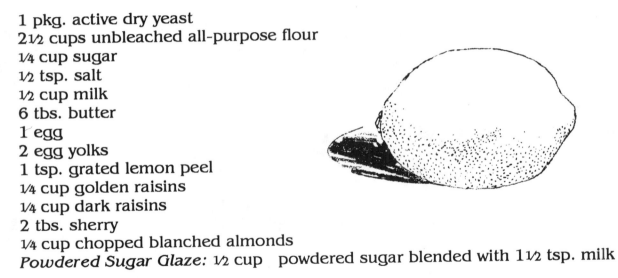

Combine yeast, 1 cup flour, sugar and salt in a large bowl. Heat milk and butter until very warm (approximately 125°). Pour into dry ingredients and beat until smooth. Beat in egg, egg yolks and lemon peel. Gradually add remaining flour, beating well after each addition. Soak raisins in sherry. Add to dough along with almonds. Turn dough out on a lightly floured board and knead until smooth and satiny. Place in a greased bowl and butter top of dough lightly. Cover with a clean kitchen towel and let rise in a warm place until doubled in size, about 1½ hours.

Turn out on a lightly floured board and knead gently a few times. Butter a 2-pound coffee can. Fold a doubled sheet of foil around top of can to extend it 2 inches. Shape dough into a ball and place in can. Loosely cover top of can with plastic wrap or foil. Let dough rise in a warm place until doubled in size, or until dough almost reaches the top of the can. Bake in a preheated 350° oven 50 minutes, or until skewer inserted in the center comes out clean and the loaf sounds hollow when thumped. Let cool on a rack. Spread frosting over top of dough and let it drizzle down sides. To serve, cut off frosted top and place in the center of a board. Cut remaining loaf lengthwise, then in crosswise slices and arrange on board around top.

CHOCOLATE STREUSEL EASTER BREAD   Makes 2

It wouldn't be Easter at home without this chocolate-streusel-filled bunny bread. It was a specialty first created at Sunset Magazine and published years ago. Over the years the dough varies and the chocolate filling increases by popular demand, but the whimsical shape stays the same. One batch of dough makes both a rabbit and duck shape with the directions that follow, but somehow the bunny rabbit is the favorite design of children of all ages. If desired, bake the bread a day or two in advance; then wrap in foil and reheat in a 350° oven for 20 minutes or until heated through.

2 pkgs. active dry yeast
½ cup lukewarm water
½ cup butter
½ cup sugar
1 tsp. salt
1 tsp. vanilla
4 eggs

1½ cups milk
5 to 6 cups unbleached all-purpose
  flour or bread flour
Chocolate Streusel Filling
1 cup chopped pecans
Powdered Sugar Glaze

Sprinkle yeast into warm water and let stand until dissolved. Beat butter until creamy and beat in sugar, salt, vanilla and eggs. Heat milk until lukewarm and mix in. Add yeast mixture. Gradually mix in flour, adding enough to make a soft dough and beating until smooth. Turn out on a floured board and knead until smooth and no longer sticky. If necessary, knead in additional flour. Place in a bowl, cover top with a towel, and let rise in a warm place until doubled in bulk, about 1½ hours.

Turn out dough on a floured board and knead lightly. Divide in half to prepare one bunny and one duck. For each piece of dough: roll out dough 8 inches wide, 54 inches long and ¼-inch thick. Sprinkle half the *Chocolate Streusel Filling* evenly over it, covering to within 1 inch of edges, and sprinkle with pecans. Roll up like a jelly roll from a long side and pinch ends to seal. Holding one end of dough, twist it a dozen times to make a rope. Then shape as follows:

Bunny. Cut a 4-inch length off each end of dough rope for ears. Cut two 1½-inch pieces for feet. Shape remaining dough into a figure 8 on a large buttered baking sheet, using about ⅖ of dough for the head and the balance for the body. Pinch ears and feet in place.

Duck. Cut a 3-inch length off each end of dough rope. Use one for a beak, the other for feet. Shape remaining dough into a figure 8 design on a buttered baking sheet, using ⅓ of dough for head and rest for body. Pull out tail. Shape beak and feet and pinch in place.

Cover with a towel and let rise in a warm place until doubled, about 45 minutes. Bake in a 325° oven for 30 to 35 minutes, or until richly browned. While still warm, spread entire surface with *Powdered Sugar Glaze.* Serve warm, sliced into ½-inch long strips.

Chocolate Streusel Filling
1 cup sugar
⅔ cup unsifted regular all-purpose
  flour

⅓ cup butter
3 tbs. ground cocoa
2 tsp. cinnamon

Mix ingredients until crumbly.

Powdered Sugar Glaze
1½ cups powdered sugar
2 tbs. milk

1 tsp. vanilla

Mix ingredients together.

ORNAMENTAL WREATH

Makes 1 wreath

A braided wreath of bread adds a festive touch to a holiday kitchen. Decorate with ornamental fruit or papier mache mushrooms and tie with a bright bow and a sheaf of grain. This ornamental wreath keeps nicely from year to year if stored in a dry place.

1 pkg. active dry yeast
1¼ cups warm water
1 tbs. sugar
2 tbs. vegetable oil

1 tsp. salt
4 cups unbleached all-purpose flour
1 egg white, lightly beaten

Sprinkle yeast into warm water in a large mixing bowl and let stand until dissolved. Mix in sugar, oil and salt. Gradually add enough flour to make a stiff dough. Turn out on a floured board and knead thoroughly, about 10 minutes. Place in a greased bowl and butter top of dough lightly. Cover and let rise in a warm place until doubled. Punch down and let rise again until doubled. Turn out on a floured board and knead lightly. Divide into 3 pieces. Roll into strands about 25 inches long. Braid and bring ends together, forming a wreath. Place on a greased baking sheet. Let rise 20 minutes. Brush with egg white and bake in a preheated 425° oven 10 minutes. Reduce heat to 300° and bake 1 hour longer or until loaf is dry throughout. Let cool and decorate.

DANISH KRINGLER

In Denmark, this holiday bread is often pretzel-shaped and delectably filled with almond paste.

6 tbs. soft butter
1½ cups unbleached all-purpose
  flour
½ pkg. active dry yeast
2 tbs. warm water
¼ cup light cream or half-and-half
1 egg

2 tbs. sugar
¼ tsp. salt
Almond Paste Filling
1 egg white, lightly beaten
granulated sugar for topping
2 tbs. sliced almonds

Beat butter and 2 tbs. flour until blended. With a spatula, spread it into a 4-x-8-inch rectangle on a sheet of waxed paper and chill. Sprinkle yeast into warm water in a large mixing bowl and let stand until dissolved. Heat cream just until warm and add to yeast. Mix in egg, sugar and salt. Beat until smooth. Gradually add remaining flour and beat until smooth. Turn out on a lightly floured board and knead until smooth and satiny. Roll out into an 8-inch square. Place the chilled butter mixture in the center of dough. Remove paper. Fold dough over chilled mixture from both sides, then fold in thirds. Roll out into a 6-x-12-inch rectangle. Repeat folding and rolling twice more. Wrap in waxed paper and chill 30 minutes. Roll into a 6-x-24-inch rectangle. Spread *Almond Paste Filling* down the center of dough. Fold dough from each side to cover it. Place on a lightly greased baking sheet and shape into a pretzel. Flatten lightly with a rolling pin. Cover with a towel and let rise at room temperature until doubled. Brush top with egg white. Sprinkle with sugar and sliced almonds. Bake in a preheated 375° oven 20 to 25 minutes, or until golden brown.

Almond Paste Filling

½ cup almond paste
2 tbs. butter
1 egg white

¼ cup shortbread or sugar cookie
  crumbs

Beat ingredients together.

DRESDEN STOLLEN

Makes 2 loaves

Germany boasts many versions of this holiday bread. Here is a famous one that ages and travels well.

¾ cup dark raisins
⅓ cup chopped citron
⅓ cup candied orange peel
¼ cup rum
1 pkg. active dry yeast
¼ cup warm water
1 cup milk
⅔ cup butter
½ cup sugar

1 tsp. salt
1 tsp grated lemon peel
½ tsp. almond extract
2 eggs
4 to 4½ cups unbleached all-
   purpose flour
½ cup chopped blanched almonds
melted butter
granulated and powdered sugar

Place raisins, citron and orange peel in a bowl, add rum and let soak 1 hour. Drain and reserve rum. Sprinkle yeast into warm water and let stand until dissolved. Heat milk and butter until butter melts. Pour into a mixing bowl. Add sugar, salt, lemon peel, drained rum and almond extract. Cool to lukewarm. Beat in eggs and dissolved yeast. Gradually add enough flour to make a soft dough. Dredge fruits in flour, add with almonds to dough and mix well. Turn out on a lightly floured board and knead until smooth and satiny. Place in a greased bowl and butter top of dough lightly. Cover with a kitchen towel and let rise in a warm place until doubled in size, about 1½ to 2 hours.

Turn out on a floured board and knead lightly. Divide in half and roll each piece into an oval about ¾-inch thick. Brush with melted butter and sprinkle with granulated sugar. Fold over lengthwise, not quite in half, so edges are within ½ inch of meeting. Place on greased baking sheets. Brush with melted butter, cover with a towel and let rise until doubled. Bake in a preheated 350° oven 40 minutes or until loaves sound hollow when thumped. Brush with butter and sprinkle generously with powdered sugar while warm.

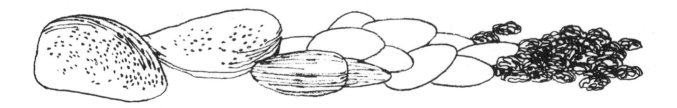

HONEY NUT STOLLEN

Makes 2 loaves

Caramelized almonds and honey fill this version of stollen.

1 pkg. active dry yeast
¼ cup warm water
⅓ cup sugar
½ tsp. salt
½ cup warm milk
⅓ cup butter, melted and cooled
2 eggs

1 egg, separated
3¼ cups unbleached all-purpose
  flour
Almond Filling
Powdered Sugar Frosting
whole or half nuts for decoration

Sprinkle yeast into warm water in a large bowl and let stand until dissolved. Stir in sugar, salt, milk, butter, whole eggs and egg yolk. Blend well. Gradually add flour and beat until smooth. Turn out on a lightly floured board and knead until smooth and no longer sticky. Place in a greased bowl and butter top of dough lightly. Cover with a clean kitchen towel and let rise in a warm place until doubled in size, about 1½ to 2 hours.

Turn out on a floured board and knead lightly. Divide in half and roll each piece into a 9 x 11-inch oval. Place on a greased baking sheet. Mound half of *Almond Filling* on one half of the length of one oval. Fold the other half over the filling and pat gently in place. Repeat with remaining filling and dough. Cover with a towel and let rise in a warm place until doubled, about 45 minutes. Brush with lightly beaten egg white. Bake in a preheated 325° oven for 30 to 35 minutes, or until golden brown and loaves sound hollow when thumped. Remove from pans and cool on wire racks. When barely warm, spread with *Powdered Sugar Frosting* and decorate with nuts. Serve sliced warm or at room temperature.

Almond Filling
1½ tbs. butter
1¼ cups slivered almonds or
 chopped pecans

2 tbs. honey or orange marmalade

In a large frying pan, heat butter and almonds or pecans. Cook until lightly browned. Cool and add honey or marmalade.

Powdered Sugar Frosting
Blend 1 cup unsifted powdered sugar with 1 tbs. milk and 1 tsp. vanilla.

GREEK EASTER BREAD (LAMBROPSOMO) Makes 1 loaf

Greeks imbed scarlet eggs in Easter bread using crosses of dough to hold them in place. This bread is named Lambropsomo because it traditionally accompanies roast lamb.

5½ cups unbleached all-purpose flour
⅔ cup sugar
½ tsp. salt
2 pkg. active dry yeast
1 cup milk
½ cup butter
1 tbs. grated lemon peel
½ tsp. anise extract, optional
4 eggs
5 hard-cooked eggs, dyed scarlet
1 egg white, slightly beaten

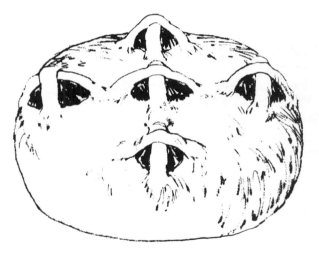

Combine 2 cups flour, sugar, salt and yeast in a mixing bowl. Heat milk and butter to about 25°. Pour over dry ingredients and beat until smooth. Add lemon peel, anise extract and eggs, one at a time. Beat well. Gradually add enough remaining flour to make a soft dough. Turn out on a floured board and knead lightly. Place in a greased bowl, cover and let rise until doubled in size.

Punch down. Turn out on a floured board and knead lightly. Cut off 1/6 of the dough to use for decoration. Shape remaining dough into a large round loaf, about 10 inches in diameter. Place on a greased baking sheet. Place 1 dyed egg in the center of the dough. Lay the other 4 around the edge, forming tips of the cross. Roll remaining dough into pencil-thin strips. Place a cross on top of each egg with the strips, pressing the end of the strips into the bread to secure the eggs. Cover and let rise until doubled in size. Brush with slightly beaten egg white. Bake in a preheated 325° oven 50 to 55 minutes, or until the loaf sounds hollow when thumped. Serve hot or let cool on a wire rack.

TSOUREKI (EASTER TWISTS)

Makes 2 twists

Another Greek holiday bread is a gala braided crown made with Lambropsomo dough, and also bedecked with scarlet eggs.

Follow the recipe for *Lambropsomo*. To shape, divide dough in half. Then divide each half into 3 pieces. Roll into strands about 24 inches long. Braid 3 strands and form into a wreath. Repeat with remaining 3 strands. Place bread wreaths on greased baking sheets. Arrange 5 hard-cooked eggs, dyed scarlet, in equal spaces around each wreath. Cover and let rise in a warm place until doubled in size. Brush the dough with slightly beaten egg white. Bake in a preheated 350° oven 25 to 30 minutes, or until golden brown.

DANISH COFFEE TWIST

The simple way in which this buttery yeast bread is cut and shaped results in its handsome pinwheel design. You have a choice of three fillings.

1 pkg. active dry yeast
¼ cup warm water
½ cup butter
6 tbs. sugar
½ tsp. salt
½ tsp. cardamom or 1 tsp. grated orange peel or 2 tsp. vanilla
3 eggs
4 cups unbleached all-purpose flour
¾ cup warm milk
Caramel, Nut or Chocolate Filling
1 egg white, beaten until frothy
sugar for topping
pecan halves, chopped filberts or slivered almonds

Sprinkle yeast into warm water and let stand until dissolved. Beat butter until creamy; beat in sugar, salt, flavoring and eggs. Add 1 cup flour and beat well. Add warm milk and dissolved yeast and beat until smooth. Gradually add remaining flour and beat until smooth. Cover and let rise until doubled, about 1½ hours.

Turn out on a floured board and knead lightly. Cut dough in half. Roll one half into a 10-x-14-inch rectangle. Spread with choice of filling. Roll up and place seam side down on a buttered baking sheet. Repeat with remaining dough and filling. Cut through rolls to within ½ inch of the bottom at ¾-inch intervals. Pull and twist each slice to lay flat. Lay them first to one side and then to the other. Cover with a towel and let rise in a warm place until doubled, about 45 minutes. Brush loaves with egg white and sprinkle with sugar and nuts. Bake in a preheated 325° oven 30 to 35 minutes, or until golden brown. Let cool on wire racks. Serve warm, cut in 1-inch slices.

Caramel Pecan Filling

Spread each rectangle with 2 tbs. butter. Sprinkle each with ½ cup firmly packed brown sugar and ¼ cup chopped pecans. Roll.

Danish Coffee Twist continued next page

Nut Streusel Filling

1 can (8 oz.) almond paste
1/4 cup soft butter
2 tbs. sugar

1/3 cup finely chopped filberts,
  almonds or pecans
1 egg

Mix ingredients together; beat until smooth. Spread half on each rectangle. Roll up.

Chocolate Streusel Filling

1/2 cup sugar
1/4 cup unbleached all-purpose flour
2 tbs. butter

1 1/2 tbs. unsweetened ground cocoa
1/2 tsp. cinnamon

Mix ingredients together until crumbly. Spread half of mixture on each rectangle. Roll up.

ITALIAN EASTER DOVE (COLOMBA DI PASQUA)

Golden with egg yolks and butter, this sweet bread resembles pound cake.

1 pkg. active dry yeast
1/4 cup warm water
1/2 cup butter
1/2 cup sugar
6 egg yolks
1/2 tsp. salt
3/4 cup warm milk

1 tsp. grated lemon peel
2 tsp. vanilla
4 1/4 cups all-purpose flour
Almond Paste Topping
1 egg white, lightly beaten
granulated sugar
1/4 cup sliced almonds

Sprinkle yeast into warm water. Let stand until dissolved. Beat butter until creamy. Beat in sugar, egg yolks and salt. Stir in warm milk, lemon peel, vanilla and dissolved yeast. Blend in 2 cups flour and beat 5 minutes. Gradually beat in remaining flour with a heavy duty mixer or wooden spoon. Turn out on a lightly floured board and knead until smooth. Place in a greased bowl and butter top of dough lightly. Cover with a towel and let rise until doubled in size, about 1 1/2 to 2 hours.

Turn dough out on a floured board and knead lightly. Divide into 4 equal pieces. Roll one piece into an oval, about 4 x 9 inches, for the wings. Lay across the width of a large baking sheet. Roll another piece into a triangle about 4 inches wide at the base and 9 inches long. Place like a cross over the wings. Holding the triangle at the center, twist it over once and press the base down for the tail. Pull out a beak with your fingers. With a sharp knife, score the tail to resemble feathers. Repeat each step with remaining dough to make a second dove. Cover and let rise in a warm place until doubled in size. Spread *Almond Paste Topping* over wings and tail. Brush egg white over entire surface of doves. Sprinkle wings and tail with sugar and almonds. Bake in a preheated 325° oven 45 to 50 minutes, or until browned.

Almond Paste Topping

1 egg white
⅓ cup almond paste
2 tbs. sugar

Beat ingredients together.

JEWISH CHALLAH

Makes 1 braid

Saffron lends a golden hue to this festive egg bread.

1 pkg. active dry yeast
5 cups unbleached all-purpose flour
  or bread flour
1 tsp. salt
⅓ cup sugar
1¼ cups very warm water (125°)

⅓ cup soft butter or vegetable oil
2 eggs
pinch of saffron or few drops yellow
  food coloring
1 egg yolk blended with 1 tbs. milk
1 tbs. sesame seeds

Combine yeast, 1½ cups flour, salt and sugar together in a mixing bowl. Stir. Pour in water and beat until smooth. Mix in butter, eggs and saffron or food coloring. Gradually add enough remaining flour to make a soft dough. Turn out on a floured board and knead until dough is smooth and elastic. Place in a greased bowl. Butter top of dough lightly and cover with a clean kitchen towel. Let rise in a warm place until doubled in size, about 1½ hours.

Punch dough down. Turn out on a floured board and knead lightly. Divide dough into 4 equal pieces. Roll each to form a strand about 20 inches long. Place the 4 strands lengthwise on a greased baking sheet. Pinch top ends together and braid as follows: pick up the strand on the right, bring it over the next one, under the third, and over the fourth. Repeat, always starting with strand on right, until braid is complete. Cut enough dough off ends to make ¾ cup. Tuck ends under and pinch to seal. Roll reserved dough into a strip about 18 inches long. Divide into 3 strands and make a small 3-strand braid. Lay on top of large braid, cover and let rise until doubled. Brush egg yolk mixture evenly over braids and sprinkle with sesame seeds. Bake in a preheated 350° oven 35 minutes, or until loaf sounds hollow when thumped.

RUSSIAN KRENDL

Makes 1 loaf

Sautéed apples, prunes and apricots hide within this pretzel-shaped loaf.

1 pkg. active dry yeast
¼ cup warm water
½ cup milk
¼ cup butter
2 tbs. sugar
1 tsp. vanilla
½ tsp. salt
3 egg yolks

3 cups unbleached all-purpose flour
Fruit Filling
Lemon Frosting
1 tbs. melted butter
2 tbs. sugar
½ tsp. cinnamon
2 tbs. sliced almonds

Sprinkle yeast into warm water and let stand until dissolved. Heat milk and butter until lukewarm. Pour over sugar in a mixing bowl. Stir in vanilla, salt, egg yolks and dissolved yeast and beat until smooth. Gradually add enough flour, beating until smooth after each addition, to make a soft dough. Turn out on a lightly floured board and knead until smooth. Place in a greased bowl, butter top of dough lightly and cover with a clean kitchen towel. Let rise in a warm place until doubled in size, about 1½ hours. Meanwhile prepare *Fruit Filling* and *Lemon Frosting*. Turn dough out on a floured board and knead lightly. Roll out into a rectangle about 9 inches wide and 28 inches long. Spread with melted butter. Mix sugar and cinnamon and sprinkle over butter. Spread on *Fruit Filling*. Roll up, starting with the 28-inch side. Pinch edges to seal and place on a greased baking sheet. Form into a stylized pretzel-shape by bringing one end over the other. Then tuck ends under center of roll. Flatten slightly, cover with a towel and let rise in a warm place until brown. Let cool slightly. Spread with *Lemon Frosting* and sprinkle with almonds while loaf is still warm.

Fruit Filling

4 Golden Delicious or Pippin apples
  peeled, cored and thinly sliced
1 tbs. butter

2 tbs. sugar
1/3 cup chopped pitted prunes
1/3 cup chopped dried apricots

Heat butter and sugar in a large frying pan. Add apples and cook over medium high heat until just tender. Add prunes and apricots and sauté until warm.

Lemon Frosting

2 tsp. melted butter
1 tsp. lemon juice

3/4 cup powdered sugar

Beat ingredients together. Add a few drops hot water if necessary to thin to a smooth, runny consistency.

GREEK CHRISTMAS BREAD (CHRISTOPSOMO)

Makes 1 loaf

This pretty holiday bread is topped with a decorative cross.

2 pkg. active dry yeast
1/2 cup warm water
1 cup butter
3/4 cup sugar
4 eggs
1 egg, separated
1/2 cup milk
2 tsp. crushed anise seed
1 tsp. salt
5 1/2 cups unbleached all-purpose flour
3/4 cup chopped walnuts or pecans, optional
9 walnut or pecan halves

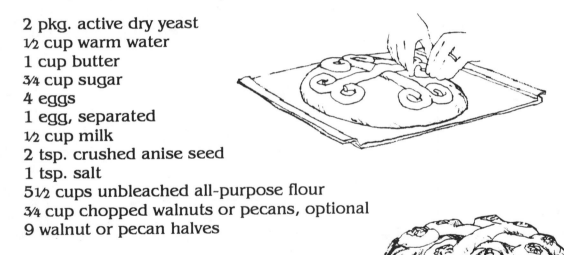

Sprinkle yeast into warm water and let stand until dissolved. Beat butter until creamy and blend in sugar, eggs and egg yolk. Heat milk with anise seed until lukewarm and add to creamed mixture along with salt. Gradually add half of the flour and beat hard 5 minutes. Gradually add remaining flour using a heavy duty electric mixer or wooden spoon. Mix in chopped nuts, if desired. Turn dough out on a lightly floured board and knead until smooth and satiny, about 10 minutes. Place dough in a greased bowl. Butter top lightly and cover with a clean kitchen towel. Let rise in a warm place until doubled, about 1½ hours.

Turn dough out on a floured board and knead lightly. Pinch off 2 pieces of dough, each about 3 inches in diameter. Set aside. Shape remaining ball of dough into a smooth flat cake, about 9 inches in diameter, and place on a greased baking sheet. Roll each of the small balls into a 14-inch rope. Cut a 5-inch slash in the end of each. Cross ropes on the center of the round loaf. Curl slashed sections away from center, forming a small circle. Place a walnut half in each circle and one in the center of the cross. Cover loaf with a towel and let rise in a warm place until doubled in size, about 1 hour. Brush loaf with slightly beaten egg white. Bake in a preheated 350° oven 45 minutes, or until golden brown and the loaf sounds hollow when thumped. Serve hot or let cool on a wire rack. To serve, cut in thirds across the loaf and then cut in ½-inch slices.

VIENNESE EASTER TWIST (WIENER OSTERSTRIETZEL)

This sweet, nutty Easter loaf makes a grand appearance on your breakfast, brunch or buffet table.

¾ cup milk
1 cup butter
¾ cup sugar
½ tsp. salt
2 pkg. active dry yeast
½ cup warm water
1 tsp. grated lemon peel
2 eggs
1 egg, separated
5½ cups unbleached all-purpose flour
¾ cup chopped filberts or slivered blanched almonds
granulated sugar

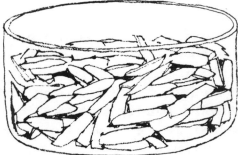

Heat milk and butter until butter melts. Pour into a large mixing bowl with sugar and salt; cool to lukewarm. Sprinkle yeast into warm water and let stand until dissolved. Stir into milk mixture. Beat in lemon peel, eggs and egg yolk. Gradually add 3 cups flour and beat 5 minutes. Add enough remaining flour to make a soft dough. Beat with a heavy duty electric mixer or wooden spoon. Mix in ½ cup nuts. Turn out on a lightly floured board and knead until smooth and satiny. Place in a greased bowl and butter top of dough lightly. Cover with a clean kitchen towel and let rise in a warm place until doubled in size.

Turn out on a floured board and knead lightly. Cut off ⅓ of the dough and set aside. Divide remaining dough into 3 strips, each about 18 inches long, and braid. Place on a greased baking sheet. Divide the smaller piece of dough into 3 strips and braid. Place on top of the larger braid. Cover with a towel and let rise in a warm place until almost doubled. Beat egg white until foamy and brush over top and sides of loaf. Sprinkle with granulated sugar and remaining nuts. Bake in a preheated 350° oven 45 to 50 minutes, or until golden brown and loaf sounds hollow when thumped. Place on a wire rack. To serve, cut in slices and serve warm or cool.

CZECHOSLOVAKIAN VANOCKA

Makes 1 braid

Pronounced VON-OOCH-KAH. For Christmas it is traditionally shaped in a 3-tiered braided loaf. You may make smaller ones if desired.

1 pkg. active dry yeast
¼ cup warm water
2 eggs
1 egg, separated
6 tbs. sugar
½ cup butter
1 cup milk

½ tsp. salt
2 tsp. grated lemon peel
4½ to 5 cups unbleached all-
  purpose flour
½ cup golden raisins
½ cup slivered blanched almonds
Lemon Glaze

Sprinkle yeast into warm water and let stand until dissolved. In a large mixing bowl, beat whole eggs and egg yolk until blended. Stir in sugar. Heat butter and milk until warm and add to egg mixture. Blend in salt, lemon peel and dissolved yeast. Gradually add enough flour to make a soft dough. Mix in raisins and almonds. Turn out on a lightly floured board and knead until smooth. Place in a greased bowl and butter top of dough lightly. Cover with a clean kitchen towel and let rise in a warm place until doubled in size, about 1½ hours.

Punch dough down. Turn out on a floured board and knead lightly. Divide in half. Divide one half into 4 pieces. Roll each into strands about 18 inches long. Braid the 4 strands as follows: lay out lengthwise. Pinch strands together at one end. Lift the right strand over the next one, under the third, and over the fourth. Repeat until all strands are braided. Tuck ends under at the finish. Divide the remaining dough in the following manner: take 2/3 of the dough and divide into 3 pieces. Make strands about 16 inches long and braid. Place on top of the 4-strand braid. Divide remaining dough in half. make 2 strands, each about 14 inches long. Twist these together and place on top. Transfer to a greased baking sheet. Cover with a towel and let rise until doubled, about 45 minutes. Beat remaining egg white until light and brush over top. Bake in a preheated 350° oven 35 to 40 minutes or until golden brown and loaf sounds hollow when thumped. Transfer to a wire rack to cool slightly. Spread with *Lemon Glaze* while still warm.

Lemon Glaze

1 cup powdered sugar
2 tsp. lemon juice

2 tsp. milk

Blend ingredients together.

PUEBLO FESTIVAL BREAD

Makes 2 loaves

New Mexico Indians bake this fanciful white bread in their beehive-shaped, outdoor ovens especially for festival days. Pull it apart for easy serving.

4 cups unbleached all-purpose flour
1 pkg. active dry yeast
2 tsp. salt

2 tbs. soft butter
1 tbs. sugar
1½ cups very warm water (125°)

Place 1½ cups flour, yeast, salt, butter and sugar in a mixing bowl. Pour in warm water and beat 2 minutes. Gradually add remaining flour, beating with a heavy duty electric mixer or wooden spoon. Turn out on a floured board and knead until smooth and satiny and no longer sticky. Place in a greased bowl and butter top of dough lightly. Cover with a clean kitchen towel and let rise in a warm place until doubled in size.

Punch dough down and turn out on a lightly floured board. Knead again to remove air bubbles. Divide dough into 2 equal pieces. With a rolling pin, roll each into a flat cake about 8 inches in diameter. Place in greased 9-inch pie pans. Then fold each in half, bringing the top half to within ½-inch of the bottom edge. With a sharp knife slash the loaf twice about ⅔ of the way through the loaf on the rounded side, making 3 equal sections. Spread the slashed sections about 1 inch apart. Cover with a towel and let rise in a warm place until doubled in size. Bake in a preheated 350° oven 35 minutes or until golden brown and loaves sound hollow when thumped.

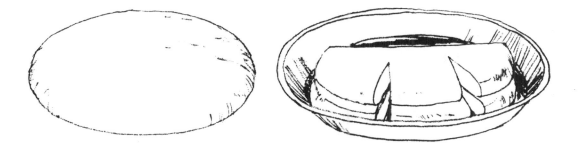

SOURDOUGH BREADS

SOURDOUGH STARTER 137
SOURDOUGH BAGUETTES 138
SOURDOUGH WHOLE WHEAT BREAD 139
THE HOUSE BREAD 140
FEATHERLIGHT ORANGE LOAVES 142
POILANE'S PEASANT BREAD 144
SOURDOUGH ENGLISH MUFFINS. 147
JIM'S SOURDOUGH ROLLS. 148
SOURDOUGH PANCAKES 148

SOURDOUGH STARTER

The zesty sourdough flavor of bread is achieved by a "starter." Several are available commercially or you may create your own. Success is not guaranteed with either, as sometimes the microorganisms simply don't respond with their characteristic sourdough flavor and leavening potential. When the starter does produce at its optimum, the results are outstanding.

2 cups lukewarm water (110°)
1 pkg. active dry yeast

2 cups unbleached all-purpose flour
½ tsp. salt

Combine water and yeast in a medium-sized crock or bowl and let stand until dissolved. Blend in flour and salt. Cover loosely with cheesecloth and place in a warm spot (ideally 80°). Each day for 4 days add ½ cup lukewarm water and ½ cup flour to feed the starter. At the end of 4 to 6 days, it should begin to give off a sour smell. Cover tightly and refrigerate. As you use the starter, replace it with equal amounts of lukewarm water and flour. It should be fed at least once a week by adding additional water and flour.

SOURDOUGH BAGUETTES

Long, slender French baguettes offer lots of crusty sourdough goodness.

1 cup lukewarm water
1 tbs. sugar
2 tbs. melted butter or vegetable oil
1 tbs. salt
1 cup sourdough starter, page 137

½ tsp. baking soda
4½ cups unbleached all-purpose
   flour
1 egg white, lightly beaten

Stir water, sugar, butter and salt together in a mixing bowl. Mix in starter and soda. Gradually beat in enough flour to make a stiff dough. Turn out on a lightly floured board and knead until smooth and satiny. Place in a greased bowl, cover and let rise in a warm place until doubled in size.

Turn out on a lightly floured board and knead lightly. Divide into 3 pieces and roll each piece into a long thin roll, about 2 inches in diameter. Place on a greased baking sheet, cover and let rise until doubled. Slash the surface diagonally with a sharp knife or a razor blade and brush with egg white. Bake in a preheated 375° oven 30 to 35 minutes or until golden brown and loaves sound hollow when thumped.

SOURDOUGH WHOLE WHEAT BREAD

Makes 2 loaves

Sourdough tang permeates this wholesome whole grain bread.

1 pkg. active dry yeast
3 cups unsifted whole wheat flour
4 cups unbleached all-purpose flour
1 cup milk
1 cup water

¾ cup sourdough starter, page 137
¼ cup honey
1 tbs. salt
3 tbs. soft butter
1 tsp. soda

Place yeast, 1 cup whole wheat flour and 1 cup all-purpose flour in a large mixing bowl. Heat milk and water to 125° and add to dry ingredients. Stir until blended. Mix in starter and beat 5 minutes. Cover bowl with plastic film and let stand in a warm place until bubbly, about 1½ to 2 hours. Stir in honey, salt, butter and soda. Gradually mix in remaining whole wheat flour and enough all-purpose flour to make a stiff dough. Turn out on a floured board and knead until smooth. Place dough in a greased bowl, cover and let rise in a warm place until doubled.

Punch down and turn out on a floured board. Knead lightly, divide in half and shape into loaves. Place in greased 9-x-5-inch loaf pans. Cover and let rise in a warm place until almost doubled. Bake in a preheated 375° oven 35 minutes or until loaves sound hollow when tapped. Remove from pans; cool on wire racks.

THE HOUSE BREAD

Makes 6 loaves

This is a favorite, versatile bread for all occasions. The European way of baking with a starter provides greater depth of flavor to bread. Standing in for part of the yeast, it also slows down the rising process slightly, and time is essential for a distinctive flavor to develop in bread. This starter can be refrigerated for a week or frozen for several weeks. It lends a slightly sour flavor to the bread.

Starter

1 tsp. active dry yeast
¼ cup warm water

1 tsp. honey
2 cups unbleached all-purpose flour

Sprinkle yeast over warm water in a large bowl and stir to dissolve. Add honey and flour; beat until smooth. Cover loosely with plastic wrap and let stand at room temperature at least 6 hours or overnight. Use ⅔ of the total amount in a recipe. To replenish, add ½ cup warm water and 1 cup flour to the starter and mix until smooth. Cover and let rise 2 to 3 hours; then refrigerate. Use within 1 week and replenish, or place in the freezer. Let thaw at room temperature for 3 hours before using.

2/3 of starter
1 pkg. active dry yeast
1/4 cup warm water
1/4 cup honey
1/4 cup olive oil, walnut oil or canola oil
1 1/2 tsp. salt
peel of 2 oranges, cut in julienne
2 1/2 cups water or whey from yogurt
  cheese

3 to 3 1/2 cups unbleached all-
  purpose flour or bread flour
3 cups whole wheat flour
3/4 cup golden raisins, snipped dried
  apricots or dates, optional
3/4 cup toasted slivered or whole
  chopped almonds or pecans

Have starter available. Sprinkle yeast into warm water and let stand until proofed. In a large mixing bowl, place honey, oil, salt, nutmeg and orange peel. Add starter and beat until smooth. Heat water or whey to about 75°, add to mixture and mix until smooth. Gradually add unbleached and whole wheat flour, adding enough to make a soft dough and beating until dough is well kneaded. Mix in raisins, if desired, and nuts. Turn out on a floured board and beat until smooth. Cover and let rise until doubled.

Turn out on a board and divide into 6 parts. Shape into round loaves. Place each dough ball into a 1-pound coffee can, cover and let rise until slightly more than double. Preheat oven to 400°. Place loaves in oven, reduce temperature to 375° and bake for 30 minutes or until loaves sound hollow when thumped. Let cool 2 to 3 minutes and remove from pans to a wire rack.

FEATHERLIGHT ORANGE LOAVES

Makes 6 loaves

The basic starter from The House Bread also enriches the flavor of this golden bread. It is ideal toasted, spread with yogurt cheese and raspberry or apricot preserves.

⅔ of starter, page 140
1 pkg. active dry yeast
¼ cup warm water
¼ cup honey
¼ cup olive oil, walnut oil or canola oil
3 eggs
1½ tsp. salt
½ tsp. nutmeg
zest of 2 oranges, cut in julienne
2½ cups water or whey from yogurt cheese
6 to 7 cups unbleached all-purpose flour or bread flour
¾ cup toasted slivered or whole chopped almonds, optional

Have starter available. Sprinkle yeast into warm water and let stand until dissolved. In a large mixing bowl, place honey, oil, eggs, salt, nutmeg and orange peel. Add starter and beat until smooth. (Replenish starter as directed.) Heat water or whey to about 75°. Pour into mixture and beat until smooth. Gradually add flour, adding enough to make a soft dough. Use a dough hook if possible and beat until dough is well kneaded. Mix in almonds, if desired. Turn out on a floured board and knead until smooth. Cover and let rise until doubled.

Turn out on a floured board and divide into 6 parts. Shape into round loaves. Place each dough ball in a greased 1-pound coffee can. Cover and let rise until slightly more than double. Preheat oven to 400°. Place loaves in oven, reduce temperature to 375° and bake for 30 minutes or until loaves sound hollow when thumped. Let cool 2 to 3 minutes; remove from pans to a wire rack.

POILANE'S PEASANT BREAD

Makes 1 large loaf

One of the most celebrated breads is Poilane's Pain de Campagne, a 2-kilogram peasant loaf that is baked in the wood-fired oven of the boulangerie built over the ruins of a 14th century Gothic abbey at 8 rue du Cherche-Midi, Paris. Visiting the shop years ago, I found perspiring young men pulling thousands of thick-crusted loaves from the hot oven daily and piling them into huge wicker baskets. Today the bread is even shipped abroad. A starter, or "chef," can be saved to create future loaves.

Starter

1 pkg. active dry yeast
½ cup warm water

½ cup lowfat milk, warmed to room temperature
1 cup whole wheat flour

Sponge

all of the starter
2 cups warm water

2 cups unbleached flour
1 cup whole wheat flour

Dough

all of the sponge

1 tbs. salt

3 cups unbleached all-purpose flour
or bread flour (approximately)

In a large bowl, stir yeast into warm water until dissolved. Add milk and whole wheat flour and mix until smooth. Cover with plastic wrap and let rise at room temperature (70°) for 24 hours. Batter will rise and fall and continue to ferment during this time.

The next day, turn back plastic wrap and pour in warm water. Stir in unbleached and whole wheat flours. Dough will be runny like a batter. Cover with plastic wrap and leave at room temperature for 24 more hours.

The next day, stir down the sponge. Add 1 cup of flour and salt. Gradually add the remaining flour to make a firm yet springy dough. Knead on a lightly floured board until smooth. Let rise at room temperature until doubled, about 1½ hours. To shape, first cut off a portion of dough, about 1 cup, to save as starter for the next batch of bread. If desired, cut off a portion for making a grape bunch or wheat stalk design. For the large piece of dough into a ball with a taut surface, about 8 inches across. Place on a greased pan, cover and let rise until tripled in volume, about 1 hour. Shortly before dough is completely risen, make top decorations, if desired.

Poilane's Peasant Bread continued next page

Grapes: Use leaf, cluster and tendrils as model. Roll dough ⅛-inch thick for leaf and cut with dough wheel, razor or sharp knife. Score veins. Pinch off 2 dozen marble-sized pieces of dough and roll into grapes. Carefully roll out long strings to resemble tendrils. Uncover loaf, lightly brush with water and position decorations forming a bunch of grapes.

Preheat oven to 425° with broiler pan placed on the bottom shelf, filled with about 1 cup hot tap water. Place loaf on middle rack of oven and bake 50 to 55 minutes or until light golden brown and hard. Remove broiler pan after about 15 minutes of baking when steam has evaporated. Makes 1 large loaf or 2 medium loaves or small rolls.

Note: If desired, shape dough into 3 loaves, place in greased 9- x-5-inch baking pans, let rise and bake in a 375° oven for 45 minutes or until loaves sound hollow when thumped.

SOURDOUGH ENGLISH MUFFINS

Makes 2 dozen

These cornmeal-coated muffins are baked on a griddle until golden brown.

1 cup sourdough starter, page 137
2 cups milk
4½ cups unbleached all-purpose
  flour

2 tbs. sugar
1½ tsp. salt
1 tsp. soda
cornmeal

In a large mixing bowl, combine starter, milk and 4 cups flour. Mix well with a wooden spoon. Cover loosely and let stand at room temperature 8 hours or overnight. Mix together remaining ½ cup flour with sugar, salt and soda. Sprinkle over dough and mix in. Turn stiff dough out on a floured board and knead a few minutes or until no longer sticky. Roll out dough ¾-inch thick. Cut into rounds with a 3-inch cutter. Place 1 inch apart on a baking sheet sprinkled with cornmeal. Dust more cornmeal on top. Cover and let rise in a warm place until doubled. Bake on a lightly greased griddle at 275° 8 to 10 minutes on a side, turning once. Serve warm or split and toast.

SOURDOUGH PANCAKES

Makes 2½ dozen pancakes

Start these pancakes the night before so they"ll be ready to bake the next morning.

½ cup sourdough starter, page 137
2 cups milk
2 cups unbleached all-purpose flour
2 eggs

2 tbs. sugar
½ tsp. salt
1 tsp. soda

Combine starter, milk and flour in a large mixing bowl. Mix until blended. Cover and let stand in a warm place 8 hours, or overnight. Add eggs, sugar, salt and soda. Beat until blended. Pour batter into 3-inch cakes on a lightly greased hot griddle. Cook until golden brown on both sides.

JIM'S SOURDOUGH ROLLS

Makes 3 dozen rolls

Prepare basic *Sourdough Pancake* batter as directed. Mix in 1 tsp. salt and enough flour (approximately 2½ to 3 cups) to make a stiff dough. Turn out on a floured board and knead until smooth. Place in a greased bowl, cover and let rise until doubled in size. Turn dough out on a floured board and roll out about ¾-inch thick. Cut out with a biscuit cutter and dip each roll in melted butter. Place in a greased pan, about 1 inch apart. Cover and let rise until doubled. Bake in a preheated 375° oven 25 to 30 minutes, or until golden brown.

DESSERT BREADS

BUNDT COFFEECAKE 150
GERMAN HONEY BEE CAKE 152
SAVARIN WITH FRUIT 154
CRISS-CROSS COFFEECAKE 156
RUM BABA 157
CHEESE-FILLED COFFEE RING 158
HONEY-GLAZED SPIRAL BREAD 160
VERONA LOAF 162
FRENCH GALETTE 164
CHOCOLATE LOAVES 166
KUGELHOPF 168

BUNDT COFFEECAKE

Chocolate streusel swirls inside this tender decorative fluted coffeecake.

1 pkg. active dry yeast
1/4 cup warm water
1/2 cup sugar
2 egg yolks
1/2 tsp. salt
1 tsp. vanilla
1/4 cup milk
1/2 cup sour cream
2/3 cup butter
3 cups unbleached all-purpose flour
2 tbs. melted butter
Chocolate Streusel
Orange Glaze: 1 cup powdered sugar blended
 with 4 tsp. orange juice

150 DESSERT BREADS

Sprinkle yeast into warm water in a large mixing bowl and let stand until dissolved. Add sugar, egg yolks, salt and vanilla. Heat milk and sour cream to lukewarm and stir into yeast mixture. Cut butter into 2½ cups flour until the mixture has a coarse crumb-like consistency. Add to yeast mixture and stir until blended. Gradually add remaining flour, mixing until smooth. Turn out on a floured board and knead a few minutes until dough is smooth and no longer sticky. Place in a greased bowl and butter top of dough lightly. Roll out into a rectangle about 12 x 16 inches. Spread with melted butter and sprinkle with *Chocolate Streusel.* Roll up like a jelly roll. Place seam side up in a greased 9- or 10-inch bundt or tube pan. Cover with a kitchen towel and let rise in a warm place until doubled in size, about 45 minutes. Bake in a preheated 350° oven 45 to 50 minutes, or until loaf sounds hollow when thumped. Let cool on a wire rack a few minutes before removing from pan. While still warm, drizzle top of loaf with *Orange Glaze.*

Chocolate Streusel

2 tbs. butter
2 tbs. flour

½ cup brown sugar
1 tbs. unsweetened cocoa

Mix ingredients together until crumbly.

GERMAN HONEY BEE CAKE (BIENENSTICH)

Makes 1 loaf

A caramelized, toasted almond topping glazes this tender coffeecake.

⅓ cup milk
⅓ cup butter
¼ cup sugar
½ tsp. salt
1 pkg. active dry yeast
¼ cup warm water
2½ cups unbleached all-purpose flour
1 egg
1 egg yolk
1 tsp. grated lemon peel
Almond Topping

Heat milk and butter until very warm. Pour over sugar and salt in a large mixing bowl. Cool to lukewarm. Sprinkle yeast into warm water, let stand until dissolved and add to milk mixture. Beat in 1 cup flour until smooth. Add egg and egg yolk and beat until smooth. Stir in lemon peel. Gradually add enough flour to make a soft dough. Turn dough out onto a floured board and knead until smooth. Place in a greased bowl and butter top of dough lightly. Cover with a clean kitchen towel and let rise in a warm place until doubled in size, about 1½ hours.

Punch dough down. Turn out on a floured board and knead lightly. Roll into a 10-inch circle. Fit into a greased 10-inch springform pan, cover and let rise until doubled in size, about 40 minutes. Bake in a preheated 350° oven 15 minutes. Spread *Almond Topping* carefully on top. Bake 15 minutes longer or until nicely browned. Cool on a wire rack and slice.

Almond Topping

⅓ cup brown sugar
2 tbs. honey
2 tbs. butter

2 tbs. heavy cream
¾ cup sliced almonds

Boil sugar, honey, butter and cream until thickened, about 3 minutes. Add almonds.

SAVARIN WITH FRUIT

Makes 12 servings

This liqueur-drenched cake ring is enhanced by juicy strawberries and sweetened whipped cream. It makes a festive party dessert.

1 pkg. active dry yeast
1/4 cup warm water
1/2 cup butter
1/3 cup sugar
4 egg yolks
1 tsp. grated lemon peel

1 tsp. vanilla
2 cups unbleached all-purpose flour
1/2 cup warm milk
Liqueur Syrup
sweetened whipped cream

Sprinkle yeast into warm water and let stand until dissolved. Cream butter and beat in sugar and egg yolks. Add lemon peel, vanilla, dissolved yeast and 1 cup flour. Beat until smooth. Add warm milk and beat until smooth. Blend in remaining 1 cup flour and beat 5 minutes longer. Heavily butter a 2-quart, 9-inch tube pan (preferably one with a fluted design). Spoon in batter and cover with a towel. Place in a warm spot and let rise until tripled in size. Bake in a preheated 350° oven 40 minutes, or until a wooden skewer inserted in the center comes out clean. Place on a wire rack to cool in pan 5 minutes. With a skewer, prick cake many times. Spoon cooled syrup over cake. Cool in pan. To serve, turn cake ring out on a platter and fill center with berries. Accompany with a bowl of whipped cream.

Liqueur Syrup

1 cup sugar

1 cup water

1 tsp. lemon peel

¼ cup brandy or cognac

¼ cup orange-flavored liqueur

Combine sugar, water and lemon peel in a saucepan and boil, stirring, just until sugar is dissolved. Remove from heat and add brandy and orange-flavored liqueur.

RUM BABA

Follow the recipe for *Savarin with Fruit* except add ⅓ cup currants, plumped in Madeira or medium dry sherry, to the batter before spooning it into the pan. Make *Liqueur Syrup* using ½ cup rum instead of brandy and orange-flavored liqueur, and any excess Madeira or sherry left from plumping the currants. Pour over cake as directed.

CRISS-CROSS COFFEE CAKE

Makes 1 loaf

Fill and shape this loaf on the baking sheet by criss-crossing the cut strips of dough.

1 pkg. active dry yeast
¼ cup warm water
2 eggs
½ cup sugar
½ tsp. salt
1 tsp. vanilla extract
¼ cup sour cream

6 tbs. melted butter, cooled
2½ cups unbleached all-purpose
  flour
Nut Filling
1 egg white, lightly beaten
sugar for topping
sliced almonds

Sprinkle yeast into warm water and let stand until dissolved. In a large mixing bowl, beat eggs until light. Gradually beat in sugar, salt, vanilla, sour cream, butter and dissolved yeast. Add 1½ cups flour and beat 5 minutes. Beat in remaining flour using a heavy duty electric mixer or wooden spoon. Turn dough out on a floured board and knead 5 minutes. Place in a greased bowl and butter top of dough lightly. Cover with a kitchen towel and let rise in a warm place until doubled. Punch dough down and turn out on a floured board. Roll into a rectangle about 10 x 15 inches. Lay on a lightly greased baking sheet. Mark dough into 3 equal lengthwise sections. Spread filling on the center third of the dough. With a sharp knife, cut diagonal strips 1 inch apart on each of the outer 2 sections of dough, cutting almost to the filling. Overlap strips first from one side, then the other. Brush loaf with beaten egg white. Sprinkle with sugar and about 2 tablespoons sliced almonds. Cover with a towel and let rise until doubled. Bake in a preheated 350° oven for 30 minutes, or until golden brown.

NUT FILLING

1 egg, beaten until light
1/2 cup firmly packed brown sugar
3/4 cup ground almonds or filberts
   (may be lightly toasted)
3/4 cup sponge cake or sugar cooky
   crumbs

Beat ingredients together.

VARIATION: PRUNE, APRICOT OR DATE FILLING

1 1/4 cups dried pitted prunes,   1/3 cup honey
   apricots or dates   1 tsp. grated lemon peel
1 cup water

Bring ingredients to a boil. Cook, covered, 10 to 12 minutes or until fruit is tender and liquid is absorbed. Let cool.

CHEESE-FILLED COFFEE RING

Makes 1 ring

Sour cream sweet bread rings the cheesecake center of this Hungarian innovation.

1 pkg. active dry yeast
¼ cup warm water
½ cup butter
3 egg yolks
⅔ cup sugar
½ cup sour cream
¼ tsp. salt

2½ cups unbleached all-purpose
  flour
2 pkg. (3 oz. each) cream cheese
1 egg
½ tsp. vanilla
½ cup apricot jam

Sprinkle yeast into warm water and let stand until dissolved. Melt butter. In a large mixing bowl, beat egg yolks until thick and light. Blend in ⅓ cup sugar, sour cream, melted butter and salt. Stir in dissolved yeast. Gradually stir in flour, mixing to make a smooth, soft dough. Turn out on a floured board and knead 5 minutes. Place in a greased bowl and butter top of dough lightly. Cover with a clean kitchen towel and let rise in a warm place until almost doubled in size, about 1½ hours.

To make filling, beat cream cheese (warmed to room temperature) with remaining ⅓ cup sugar and egg. Blend in vanilla.

Punch dough down and turn out on a floured board. Knead a few minutes. Roll dough into a circle about 15 inches in diameter. Lay dough over a greased 1½-quart ring mold. Fit the dough carefully down into the bottom and sides of the mold, being careful not to poke holes in it. Let it hang over the outside. Pour in cheese filling. Lift outside edges of dough and lap over filling. Seal to inside ring of dough. Cut a cross in the dough which covers the center hole of ring mold. Fold each triangle formed back over the ring. Cover with a towel and let rise in a warm place until doubled in size, about 45 minutes. Bake in a preheated 350° oven 30 to 35 minutes, or until golden brown. Let cool 10 minutes; then turn out with top side down. When cool, heat jam until it flows easily and force through a wire sieve. Spoon over ring. Cut into wedges.

HONEY-GLAZED SPIRAL BREAD

Makes 2 spirals

A caramelized sheath of crunchy nuts bakes on this pinwheel of sweet bread.

1 pkg. active dry yeast
¼ cup warm water
6 tbs. butter
⅔ cup sugar
½ tsp. salt
1 tsp. grated orange peel
3 eggs
1 cup lukewarm milk
4 cups unbleached all-purpose flour
Honey Glaze
½ cup chopped walnuts or slivered almonds

Stir yeast into warm water and let stand until dissolved. cream butter and sugar in a large mixing bowl. Beat in salt, orange peel, eggs and milk. Blend in dissolved yeast. Add 1 cup flour and beat until smooth. Add 1½ cups flour and beat 5 minutes. Gradually add enough remaining flour to make a soft dough. Turn out on a lightly floured board and knead until smooth and satiny, about 5 to 10 minutes. Place in a greased bowl and lightly butter top of dough. Cover and let rise in a warm place until doubled in size.

Turn out on a lightly floured board and knead lightly. Divide dough in half. Using fingertips, roll each piece into a long rope about 1 inch thick. Place on a greased baking sheet and coil into a spiral. Repeat with remaining dough. Cover and let rise in a warm place until doubled in size. Spread surface with *Honey Glaze* and sprinkle with nuts. Bake in a preheated 350° oven 35 minutes, or until golden brown. Serve warm.

Honey Glaze
2 tbs. soft butter
¾ cup powdered sugar

2 tbs. honey
1 egg white

Beat ingredients together.

VERONA LOAF

This lemon-scented Italian loaf calls for rolling and folding firm butter slices into the dough. The result is a lovely tender loaf with buttery pockets throughout.

3¼ cups unbleached all-purpose
  flour
⅓ cup sugar
½ tsp. salt
1 tbs. grated lemon peel
1 pkg. active dry yeast

¾ cup very warm water (125°)
½ cup butter
3 eggs
1½ tsp. vanilla extract
1 egg white, lightly beaten
granulated sugar for topping

Place 1 cup flour, sugar, salt, lemon peel and yeast in a large mixing bowl. Gradually add very warm water and beat until smooth. Beat in ¼ cup butter, cut in small pieces. Beat at medium speed for 2 minutes. Add eggs, vanilla and ½ cup flour. Beat hard 2 minutes longer. Gradually add enough remaining flour to make a soft dough. Turn out on a lightly floured board and knead until smooth and satiny. Place in a greased bowl and butter top of dough lightly. Cover with a clean kitchen towel and let rise in a warm place until doubled, about 45 minutes.

Punch dough down and turn out on a floured board. Knead lightly and roll into a rectangle about ½-inch thick. Cut 2 tablespoons butter into small pieces.

Place in center 1/3 of dough. Fold 1/3 of the dough over butter and place remaining butter, cut in pieces, on top. Bring remaining 1/3 of the dough over to cover butter. Roll out making a strip 18 inches long. Fold into thirds and wrap loosely in waxed paper. Refrigerate 20 minutes. Repeat, rolling dough into 18-inch strip, folding into thirds and chilling 2 times. On a floured board divide dough in half. Stretch top of each piece, pulling it underneath to form a ball. Place in 2 greased 8-inch round cake pans. Cover and let rise in a warm place until doubled in size, about 35 minutes. Brush with lightly beaten egg white and sprinkle with sugar. Bake in a preheated 350° oven 30 to 35 minutes, or until loaves sound hollow when thumped. Remove from pans and cool slightly. Serve warm with sweet butter.

FRENCH GALETTE
(DESSERT TART PEROUGES STYLE)

Makes 8 servings

This big pizza-like sweet bread makes a spectacular dessert. Serve it piping hot from the oven, short-cake style, with fresh berries and cream.

1 pkg. active dry yeast
6 tbs. warm water
½ cup soft butter
6 tbs. sugar
1 egg

1 tsp. grated lemon peel
½ tsp. salt
1¾ cups unbleached all-purpose
 flour

Sprinkle yeast into warm water in a large mixing bowl and let stand until dissolved. Beat in ¼ cup butter, 2 tablespoons sugar, egg, lemon peel and salt. Gradually add enough flour to make a soft dough. Beat well. Turn out on a floured board and knead until satiny and no longer sticky. Place in a greased bowl and butter top of dough lightly. Cover with a clean kitchen towel and let rise in a warm place until doubled in size.

Punch dough down and turn out on a floured board. Knead lightly. Roll out into a 15-inch circle and place in a greased 14-inch pizza pan or on a baking sheet. Form a rim around the edge. Spread with remaining ¼ cup soft butter and sprinkle with remaining ¼ cup sugar. Let stand in a warm place 20 minutes. Bake in a preheated 500° oven 6 minutes or until golden brown. Serve at once, hot, cut into pie-shaped wedges. If desired, accompany with vanilla-flavored whipped cream or ice cream and fresh berries or sliced peaches.

CHOCOLATE LOAVES

Makes 2 loaves

Here is a bread for chocolate lovers.

1 pkg. active dry yeast
¼ cup warm water
1¾ cups milk, heated to lukewarm
½ cup butter
¾ cup sugar
3 eggs
5 cups unbleached all-purpose flour
½ cup unsweetened cocoa
1 tsp. salt
1 tsp. vanilla extract
¾ cup chopped walnuts or pecans
Powdered Sugar Glaze

Sprinkle yeast into warm water and let stand until dissolved. Cream butter in a large mixing bowl and beat in sugar and eggs. Stir in milk and dissolved yeast. Add 2 cups flour and beat until smooth. Mix in cocoa, salt and vanilla.

166 DESSERT BREADS

Add enough remaining flour to make a soft dough. Stir in nuts. Turn out on a lightly floured board and knead until smooth and satiny. Place in a greased bowl and butter top of dough lightly. Cover with a clean kitchen towel and let rise in a warm place until doubled in size.

Turn dough out on a lightly floured board and knead until smooth. Divide in half and shape into 2 round loaves. Place in greased 8- or 9-inch round cake pans. Cover with a towel and let rise in a warm place until doubled in size, about 45 minutes. Bake in a preheated 350° oven 35 to 40 minutes or until loaves sound hollow when thumped. Remove from pans and let cool on a wire rack. Spread with *Powdered Sugar Glaze.*

Powdered Sugar Glaze
1½ cups powdered sugar
1½ tbs. milk

1 tsp. vanilla or rum

Beat ingredients together.

KUGELHOPF

The spelling of this yeast-raised coffee ring cake will vary through the European countries, but the decorative fluted tube shape is always the same.

1 pkg. active dry yeast
¼ cup lukewarm water
⅓ cup golden raisins
2 tbs. dry white wine or rum
½ cup butter
⅓ cup sugar
4 egg yolks or 2 whole eggs

1 tsp. grated lemon zest
1 tsp. vanilla
2 cups unbleached all-purpose flour
½ cup light cream
12 whole blanched almonds
powdered sugar

Sprinkle yeast into warm water and let stand until dissolved. Plump raisins in wine or rum. Beat butter until creamy; beat in sugar and egg yolks. Add lemon peel and vanilla. Mix in dissolved yeast and 1 cup of flour and beat until smooth. Add cream and beat until smooth. Add remaining 1 cup flour and beat well, about 5 minutes longer. Mix in raisins and remaining wine and beat again.

Butter a deep 9-inch tube pan or mold, preferably one with a fluted design, and arrange almonds in the bottom. Spoon in batter, cover and let rise until tripled in size. Bake in a preheated 350° oven for 40 minutes, or until a wooden skewer inserted in center comes out clean. Remove from pan and cool on a wire rack. Dust with powdered sugar.

INDEX

Anadama bread 26

Baking 10
Basic white bread 14
Bear claws 80
Bowknots 64
Braid rolls 65
Bread that doesn't rise 10
Bread that rises too much 11
Brioche 40
  braid 41
  cheese braid 41
  filbert rounds 43
  mousseline 44
  onion sandwiches 44
  ring 46
  sandwich star 48
  with chocolate sauce 45
Buccellati 99
Bundt coffeecake 150

Caramel
  cinnamon twists 72
  pecan rolls 76
Cheese
  cheddar bread 16
  in brioche 42
  filled coffee ring 158

Chocolate
  loaves 166
  streusel Easter bread 106
Cinnamon
  rolls 79
  swirl bread 15
Cloverleaf rolls 64
Cooling 10
Coping with problems 10
Corkscrew rolls 65
Crescent rolls 64
Criss-cross coffee cake 156
Croissants 82
Czechoslovakian vanocka 132

Danish
  coffee twist 119
  kringler 110
  pastry cockscombs 80
Date pecan bread 17
Dessert bread
  bundt coffeecake 150
  cheese-filled coffee ring 158
  chocolate loaves 166
  criss-cross coffee cake 156
  French galette 164
  German honey bee cake 152
  honey-glazed spiral bread 160

  kugelhopf 168
  rum baba 155
  savarin with fruit 154
  verona loaf 162
Dessert brioche with fruit 47
Dill batter bread 56
Dinner rolls 63
Dresden stollen 112

Egg bread
  brioche 40
  brioche braid 41
  brioche cheese braid 41
  brioche filbert rounds 43
  brioche mousseline 44
  brioche onion sandwiches 44
  brioche ring 46
  brioche sandwich star 48
  brioche with chocolate sauce 45
  cheese in brioche 42
  dessert brioche with fruit 47
  dill batter bread 56
  Finnish celebration bread 58
  Holland brioche cakes 66
  Italian Parmesan bread 52
  monkey bread 50
  Sally Lunn 57
  sausage in brioche 42

Egg breads, continued
  Swiss cinnamon braid 60
  Turkish cheese bread 54
Eggs 6

Fat 6
Featherlight orange loaves 142
Filbert crescents 74
Finnish celebration bread 58
Flour 4
Focaccia 36
Fougasse 36
Freezing 10
French
  galette 164
  -style white bread 16
  -style crusty rolls 84
Frosted pinwheels 78
Fruit bread
  Czechoslovakian vanocka 132;
  date pecan bread 17
  dessert brioche with fruit 47
  Dresden stollen 112
  Grammy's orange bread 28
  kulish 104
  panettone 100
  raisin bread 15
  Russian krendl 126
Fruits 6

German honey bee cake 152

Glazes 9
Grammy's orange bread 28
Greasing bowl 8
Greek Christmas bread 128
Greek Easter bread 116

Hand kneading 7
Holland brioche cakes 66
Honey nut stollen 114
Honey-glazed spiral bread 160
Hot cross buns 68
House bread 140

Ingredients 4
International holiday bread
  buccellati 99
  chocolate streusel Easter bread
    106
  Czechoslovakian vanocka 132
  Danish coffee twist 119
  Danish kringler 110
  Dresden stollen 112
  Greek Christmas bread 128
  Greek Easter bread 116
  honey nut stollen 114
  Italian Easter dove 122
  Jewish challah 124
  kulich 104
  ornamental wreath 109
  panettone 100
  Portuguese sweet bread 102

pueblo festival bread 134
Russian krendl 126
tsoureki 118
Viennese Easter twist 130
Introduction 1
Italian
  Easter dove 122
  Parmesan bread 52
  salt sticks 95
Jewish challah 124
Kugelhopf 168
Kulich 104

Leavening 5
Lebanese anise buns 70
Liquids 6

Machine kneading 8
Mexican pan dulce 92
Mixed nut bread 20
Monkey bread 50

Nut bread 30
Nuts 6

Onion buns 88
Ornamental wreath 109

Panettone 100
Parker House rolls 64
Peasant potato rounds 24
Pita 86

Pocket bread 86
Poilane's peasant bread 144
Portuguese sweet bread 102
Preliminary mixing 7
Pueblo festival bread 134
Punching down 9, 11

Quick honey white bread 13

Raisin bread 15
Rising 8
Roasted garlic loaves 22
Rolls
  bowknots 64
  braids 65
  caramel cinnamon twists 72
  caramel pecan 76
  cinnamon 79
  cloverleaf 64
  corkscrews 65
  crescents 64
  croissants 82
  Danish pastry cockscombs 80
  dinner 63
  filbert crescents 74
  French-style crusty 84
  frosted pinwheels 78
  Holland brioche cakes 66
  Hot cross buns 68
  Italian salt sticks 95

Lebanese anise buns 70
Mexican pan dulce 92
onion buns 88
Parker House 64
pita 86
rosettes 65
sesame hamburger buns 90
Swedish almond crescents 96
Rossette rolls 65
Rum baba 155
Russian
  black bread 32
  krendl 126

Sally Lunn 57
Salt 6
San Benito House molasses
  bread 27
Sausage in brioche 42
Savarin with fruit 154
Sesame hamburger buns 90
Shaping 9
Sourdough
  baguettes 138
  English muffins 147
  featherlight orange loaves 142
  house bread 140
  pancakes 148
  Poilane's peasant bread 144
  starter 137

whole wheat bread 139
Sugar 6
Swedish almond crescents 96
Swiss cinnamon braid 60

Testing 9
Testing for lightness 9
Time limitations 11
Tips and techniques 7
Tsoureki 118
Turkish cheese bread 54

Variety bread 34
Vegetable breads
  peasant potato rounds 24
  variety bread 34
Verona loaf 162
Viennese Easter twist 130

Whole grain bread
  anadama bread 26
  cheese wheat bread 19
  health bread 19
  Russian black bread 32
  San Benito House molasses
    bread 27
  sourdough whole wheat bread 139
  whole wheat bread 15
  whole wheat coffee can bread 18
Whole wheat bread 15

SERVE CREATIVE, EASY, NUTRITIOUS MEALS WITH NITTY GRITTY® COOKBOOKS

Extra-Special Crockery Pot Recipes
Cooking in Clay
Marinades
Deep Fried Indulgences
Cooking with Parchment Paper
The Garlic Cookbook
Flatbreads From Around the World
From Your Ice Cream Maker
Favorite Cookie Recipes
Cappuccino/Espresso: The Book of
  Beverages
Indoor Grilling
Slow Cooking
The Best Pizza is Made at Home
The Well Dressed Potato
Convection Oven Cookery
The Steamer Cookbook
The Pasta Machine Cookbook
The Versatile Rice Cooker

The Dehydrator Cookbook
The Bread Machine Cookbook
The Bread Machine Cookbook II
The Bread Machine Cookbook III
The Bread Machine Cookbook IV
The Bread Machine Cookbook V
Worldwide Sourdoughs From Your
  Bread Machine
Recipes for the Pressure Cooker
The New Blender Book
The Sandwich Maker Cookbook
Waffles
The Coffee Book
The Juicer Book
The Juicer Book II
Bread Baking (traditional), revised
No Salt, No Sugar, No Fat
  Cookbook

Cooking for 1 or 2
Quick and Easy Pasta Recipes
The 9x13 Pan Cookbook
Chocolate Cherry Tortes and
  Other Lowfat Delights
Low Fat American Favorites
Now That's Italian!
Fabulous Fiber Cookery
Low Salt, Low Sugar, Low Fat
  Desserts
Healthy Cooking on the Run
Healthy Snacks for Kids
Muffins, Nut Breads and More
The Wok
New Ways to Enjoy Chicken
Favorite Seafood Recipes
New International Fondue Cookbook

Write or call for our free catalog.
BRISTOL PUBLISHING ENTERPRISES, INC.
P.O. Box 1737, San Leandro, CA 94577
(800) 346-4889; in California (510) 895-4461